Honiton Lace
— a practical guide

Cynthia Voysey

Bishopsgate Press Ltd.
37 Union Street, London SE1 1SE

ACKNOWLEDGEMENTS

I would like to thank my daughters Sharon Tait and Lorraine Pearce for helping with the typing of the script. Thanks also to my husband for his helpful comments on my work but mostly for his understanding of the disruption to domestic life while this book was in progress.

Gratitude to my Mother, who although she did not teach me to make lace, did interest me at a very early age in many other crafts.

British Library Cataloguing in Publication Data

Voysey, Cynthia
    Honiton lace.
    746.22

ISBN 1 85219 057 4

All enquiries and requests relevant to this title should be sent to the publisher, Bishopsgate Press Ltd., 37, Union Street, London, SE1 1SE

Printed in Great Britain by
Whitstable Litho Printers Ltd., Whitstable, Kent

CONTENTS

INTRODUCTION

Lace has been made in East Devon since the 17th century. By the early 18th century this closely resembled Brussels lace. Changes in fashion at the end of the 18th century led to a decline in this type of lace; less heavily patterned laces were preferred.

In the early 19th century Heathcoates moved their machine-net factory from Nottingham to Devon. This provided a cheap foundation for veils and collars. Motifs and edging could be made and applied to machine net.

Royal patronage early in the 19th century helped the Honiton lace industry although when Queen Victoria had flounce and trimmings, which were later used for her wedding dress, and also a wedding veil from Jane Bidney at Beer it was difficult to find enough skilled lace makers to complete the order. There were at this time a few people who organised lacemakers and some excellent lace was made under their guidance. The cottage industry however produced a lot of very poor work. Lace machines were now able to imitate the most intricate laces and hand workers could not compete with them. After the first world war very little lace was made professionally.

Honiton lace is now, in the 20th century, mostly made as a hobby. It is very popular and although still made mainly in Devon its popularity has spread not only in this country but also abroad. Honiton lace teachers from Devon have been invited to teach in many countries including America, Finland, New Zealand and Europe. Although fine and intricate, lacemaking is a very relaxing hobby and because of the way it is made piece by piece Honiton lace is full of possibilities for anyone who is artistic. Each flower is individually worked and joined one to the other as the work progresses.

The thread used is very fine though not as fine as the thread used in the best lace in the 19th century, which is no longer obtainable. The finest thread now made is an Egyptian gassed cotton of 170 thickness. A slightly thicker thread of 120 is used by most lace makers starting to learn to make Honiton Lace.

A very pleasurable side of lace making is the beautiful bobbins with which it is made. Antique ones are rarely available but these were often decorated with incised patterns filled with black and red sealing wax. Modern bobbins are often made from hardwood of great variety and some are spliced with one, two or more woods. It is also possible to buy hand painted bobbins.

This book is written in the hope it will bring a great number of people to know the pleasure of lacemaking.

FOREWORD

The first part of this book details the equipment needed to make Honiton Lace. It is possible to purchase this from lace suppliers but instructions are given for making a pillow, bobbin case and cover cloths. Bobbins can be made from dowel but they must be very well finished as the fine thread would catch on any rough parts and break.

The remainder of the book contains four patterns which include most of the basic techniques used in Honiton Lace. There are also two simple patterns which include techniques from these four.

The last section gives line diagrams and written instructions for ten filling stitches.

Many tips are given throughout to help perfect tension and techniques.

GLOSSARY

Coarse thread	—	a thicker thread used inside the pinhole edge of the lace. (Often called a Gimp in other laces.)
Downrights	—	(or passives), these are the bobbins, between the pins which remain hanging in the same position they never weave too and fro.
Edge pairs.	—	these are the two pairs of runners left at the edge of the lace while the third pair are the runners working the row.
Filling.	—	a fancy stitch to fill an area within a design
Half stitch.	—	one of the two basic stitches. It gives an open mesh-like effect.
Half stitch plait.	—	a series of half stitches made with two pairs of bobbins to make a bar. This is often used to take pairs from one block of a filling to another.
Leadwork.	—	(or cutwork) a woven flat-ended bar or square, made by weaving one bobbin back and forth between three others. Also called a tally, and when pointed at each end a wheatear or leaf in East Midlands lace.
Purl.	—	(picot) a decorative loop used on the outside edge of a veil or handkerchief etc. They are also used to decorate bars (or brides) when used as a filling.
Runners.	—	(or weavers) are the three pairs of runners which take it in turns weaving the rows of lace.
Snatch	—	A group of 6 holes
Weaver.	—	This is the bobbin used to weave a leadwork.
Whole stitch	—	(or cloth stitch) one of the two basic stitches which resembles woven cloth.

TOOLS & EQUIPMENT

Pillow

A Honiton lace pillow is made of an unbleached calico casing filled with barley straw. For the case cut two 14in (36 cm) circles and a strip 4in (10 cm) for the gusset. With two rows of stitching for strength, machine one circle to the gusset with a ½in seam (½ cm). Join the gusset and then stitch the second circle to the other edge of the gusset leaving 5 - 6in (13 - 15 cms) open, through which to stuff the pillow.

Cut the barley straw into lengths of about 3in (8 cms) and put a handful at a time into the pillow. The pillow needs to be very hard to support the pins. Using the above measurements the pillow should weigh a minimum of 2 ¼lbs (1 kgm). It is helpful to stand on the pillow from time to time while stuffing it in order to compact the straw. The final few handfuls can be pushed in with the aid of a wooden spoon. Then the opening needs oversewing with a strong thread used double.

Bobbins

Approximately four dozen bobbins will be needed unless a large filling is to be made.

Honiton lace bobbins are best made of wood, bone is too heavy for fine thread. These are about 3¾in (9.5cm) long and ¼in (0.75cm) in diameter.

It is possible to make them from dowel but they must be well finished as any rough areas would catch on the thread and cause it to break. Bobbins are readily available from the lace suppliers in basic woods or various hardwoods, inlaid, spliced and hand-painted.

Traditionally, Honiton bobbins were made from spindlewood and fruit woods. Some had patterns incised in them which were then filled with red and black sealing wax.

Cover Cloths

These cloths are used to cover the pillow to keep the lace clean as it is being made and also to cover the pins in already completed parts of the work to prevent the working threads catching on them.

A square yard or square metre of fine polycotton is cut into four pieces. These must have their raw edges hemmed.

Traditionally dark blue has always been used but any dark *plain* material that is restful to the eyes and will show up the white thread is suitable. It is most important that this material has no loose fibres which would become woven into lace.

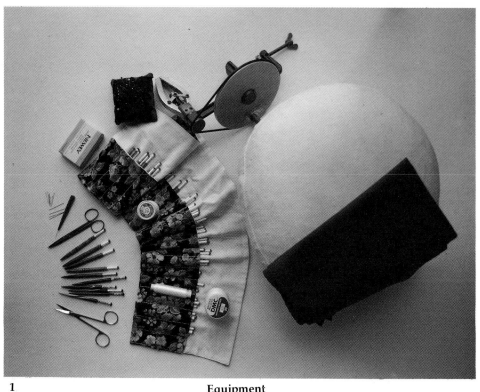

1   Equipment

Lace Pins

Honiton pins are usually 0.26 mm or 0.30 mm long and 0.53 mm thick, either yellow brass or plated. Special fine headed ones are ideal as then all the pins can be pushed down as areas of the work are completed.

Berry Pins

These glass headed pins are best for securing the cover cloths on the pillow as they are easily removed when the cloths need moving.

Needlepin

A needlepin is a piece of wood about the size of a bobbin with a needle pushed into one end, eye first. The needle needs to protrude about ½in to ¾in (1 - 2 cms) and should be slightly smaller than the pins, a size 9 is ideal. The needlepin in used for taking 'sewings' and shortening the threads on the bobbins.

Pricking Board

Small patterns can be pricked on the pillow but larger ones would be better pricked on a cork board or a polystyrene tile.

Scissors

A small sharp pair of embroidery scissors are needed for cutting off bobbins as sections of the lace are completed.
A small, loose blunt pair of scissors with points are used for joining bobbins together. (An old pair of nail scissors are ideal).

Threads

Honiton lace is traditionally one of the finest of English laces. It is usual now to make first pieces with 120/2 cotton thread and then to use finer 170/2 or 180/2. When a coarse thread is used a 50 cotton is suitable for use with a 120 thread and a 50 retours d'alsace with the 170/2 and 180/2.

Lace thread should always be kept in a cool room and stored in acid free tissue. Undue heat causes the fibres to become brittle and snap. it is therefore unwise to keep a lace pillow which is in use close to a heat source, i.e. a radiator or a fire.

Pricker

This is used for pricking the holes in the pricking card when making the pattern. It can either be a wooden one similar to a needlepin but with a shorter needle (about ½in (1.25 cms) protruding from the handle) or a pin vice can be used and should a needle break it is easier to repelace. A number 9 needle is ideal as this is smaller than the pins. If a large needle is used the pins wobble in the hole and it will not be possible to make good lace.

Pincushion

This should be small about 2in (5 cm) square or a 2in (5 cm) diameter if round. It must be lint free and filled with either sheeps wool or emery powder. It is usually attached to the pillow with a large hat pin or something similar.

Pricking Card

A special glazed card must be used for this purpose. It is essential for Honiton lace because of the constant use of the needlepin for taking 'sewings'. Anything else would break up and could get woven into the lace.

How to make a bobbin case

This should be made from a lint-free material i.e. cotton poplin or polycotton.

Cut two pieces of material 21in (52'6cm) by 12 ½in (32 cm). One of these pieces is for the lining of the bobbin case if wished, one may be of a patterned and one a plain material. Place the right sides together and machine around the edges ½in (1¼ cm) leaving a small space 2in wide (5 cm) in order to turn the case in the right way. Before doing this trim the seams and the corners. Turn in the right way and slip stitch up the opening. Press well and turn up the bottom 3½in (9 cm). Machine each pocket 1in (2½ cm) wide. Following these instructions the case will have twenty pockets. If desired the two pieces of material could be cut 20in x 17½in (50 cm x 44 cm), 3½in (9 cm) could then be turned over at the top and the bottom making double the number of pockets. Attach a length of ribbon as illustrated, approximately 24 in (60 cm) folded in half to one end of the bobbin case. When not in use roll the case from the opposite end and tie the ribbon around the roll to secure the bobbins.

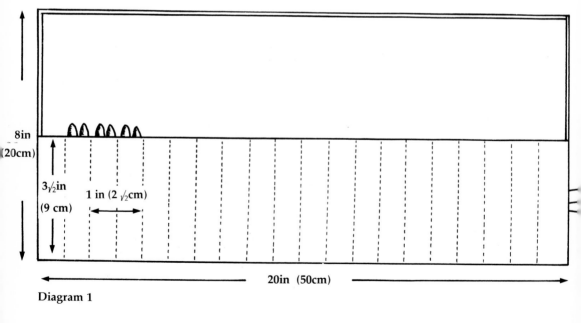

8in
(20cm)

3½in
(9 cm)

1 in (2 ½cm)

20in (50cm)

Diagram 1

12

To make a pattern

To make a pattern first photocopy the dotted pattern in the book. Cut a piece of glazed pricking card 1½in (4 cm) bigger all around than the pattern (Fig 2). Place the pattern on top of the pricking card and pin to the pillow or board through the four corners.

Take a pin vice or pricker with a number nine needle and with a pin vice held vertically, carefully prick through each dot on the pattern. A good pricking is essential as good lace cannot be made with a badly pricked pattern. When the pricking is completed remove two of the four securing pins and check all the holes have been pricked. If this is so then remove the photocopy and pin the pattern in the centre of the pillow.

N.B.   The pattern is always the reverse of the finished lace as the work is carried out on the wrong side of the lace. When completed and the pins carefully removed the lace is turned over.

Dressing the pillow

When the pattern has been placed in the centre of the pillow it is necessary to pin on the cover cloths. The area to be worked must be visible. Pin two cloths on either side of this and then a third one across the bottom as shown in the first photographs where the lace is being commenced.

2   Pattern, card, and pricker

Winding a Bobbin with Thread

Hold down the end of the thread against the shank of the bobbin with the thumb. When looking down at the head of bobbin wind the thread around it in a clockwise direction (diagram 2). When the end is secure hold the bobbin in one hand and the thread in the other and gradually half-fill the shank by turning the bobbin rather then wrapping the thread around the bobbin which affects the twisting of the thread itself.

A half-hitch must be put on all the bobbins to prevent them from unwinding when in use (diagram 3). If a bobbin is wound the wrong way the half-hitch will not hold.

To release more thread from the bobbins to lengthen them whilst working it is only necessary to twist the bobbins towards the left.

If a bobbin should become too long insert the needle pin in the loop of the half-hitch and twist the bobbin towards the right.

Diagram 2

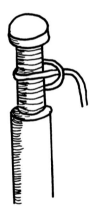

Diagram 3

"Bowing off" the Bobbins

Because Honiton lace is a non-continuous lace bobbins are constantly being cut off and joined together again to start a new section.

The easiest way to join them together is to hold a pair of bobbins in the left hand, release enough thread from them to hold over the hand and between the fourth and little finger. Take a pair of loose, blunt scissors. Put them, with the blades closed, under the threads lying over the hand. (fig 3) Bring the scissors over towards you (fig 4) and around to face your little finger. Open out the blades of the scissors and catch hold of the threads, (fig 5) close the scissors, and bring these through the loop of thread around the scissors. (fig 6) Cut the resultant loop still held between the blades and then remove the scissors and the ends of threads. This will leave the two bobbins knotted together.

This method can also be used to remove bobbins from the pillow, when a piece of lace is complete.

When the bobbins have been thus joined it is necessary to wind the knots on to one of the pair of bobbins. To do this wind off about 18in (45 cm) of thread from one bobbin. Take the other bobbin in one hand and a needlepin in the other. Insert the needlepin into the loop of the half-hitch to slacken it and wind the bobbin in an anticlockwise direction. The thread and knot will then wind on to this bobbin.

Joining the bobbins in this way means that the thread is not handled too much and so keeps clean.

It is possible of course to wind one bobbin and put a little of the thread onto a second bobbin. If using this method then the bobbins with the smaller amount of thread will replace the 'knotted' bobbins in the following working instructions.

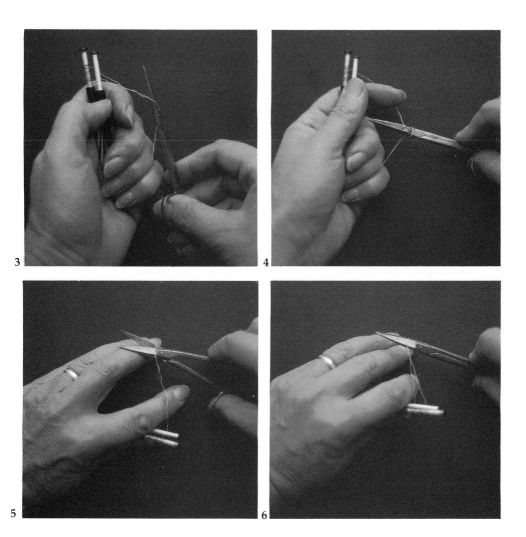

BASIC STITCHES

Whole Stitch. This is sometimes called "cloth stitch" as it makes a woven fabric.

Four bobbins are required to make the stitch and are always referred to in pairs. One pair of bobbins which will work along the entire row are called runners and one downright (or passive) pair are used with them for each stitch.

The second bobbin from the left is placed over the one to its right using the left hand, (diagram 4a). The bobbins on either side of this one are taken one in each hand and placed over the two bobbins to their left, (diagram 4b). Lastly the second bobbin from the left is now placed over the bobbin to its right, using the right hand, (diagram 4c). This stitch is worked in the

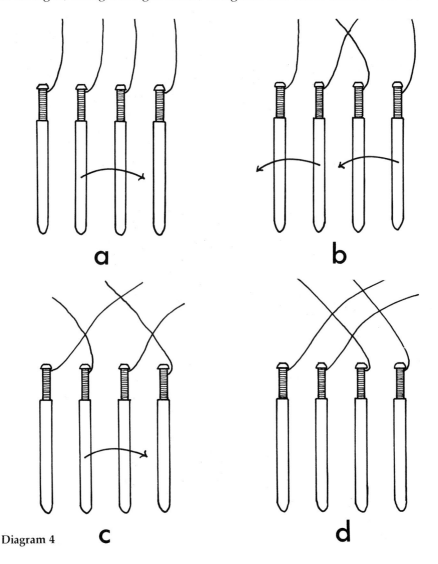

Diagram 4

same order whether working from right to left or vica versa. Diagram 4d shows the position of the threads after one complete stitch.

Half Stitch. This is the second of the two basic stitches and has a more open texture. As with whole stitch two pairs of bobbins are needed to make a stitch.

One bobbin from the left is placed over the one to its right using the left hand, (diagram 5a). The bobbins on either side of this one are taken one in each hand and are now placed over the two bobbins to the left, (diagram 5b). (Half stitch is the first two movements of whole stitch).

One bobbin instead of two, as in whole stitch, travels across the row and all the other bobbins become twisted right over left. Diagram 5c show the position of the threads after one complete stitch.

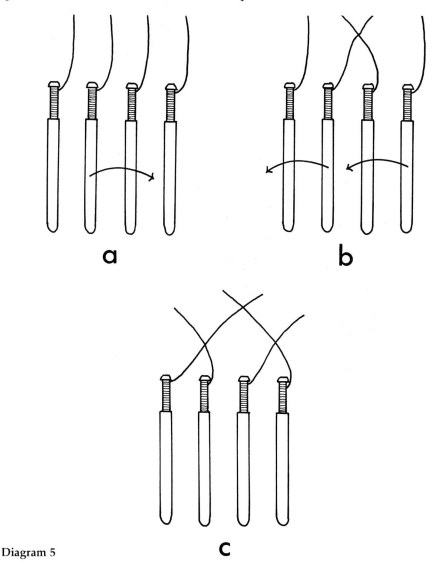

a

b

Diagram 5

c

TENSION

Good tension is essential to good lacemaking. Firstly when placing the pins in the holes they should slope slightly outwards and backwards. Sloping them outwards ensures the lace remains down on the pillow and does not rise up the pins. Sloping the pins slightly backwards makes sewing out easier. It would be impossible to do this with the pins sloping forwards as they would impede the free movement of the needlepin.

When making the edge stitches at the ends of the rows, pull up well after the whole stitch made with both pairs of runners, twist them both three times and pull up again. Make the first stitch of the row and pull up once more. This will ensure good tension on the horizontal threads and small, neat pinholes.

Moving the downright pairs across the pillow slightly while working helps to keep the vertical tension even and also prevents the threads from building up on the outside edge of the work. Do *not* however pull the coarse thread away from the pins as this will make large untidy pinholes. Every two or three rows gently pull the downright pairs but be very careful not to pull the downright pairs on the outside of a curve as they will pull away from the pins.

BROKEN THREADS

How to make a weavers knot.   (Half Hitch)

If a thread breaks a weaver's knot is made to rejoin the thread. Should this have broken close to the work it is necessary to unpick the work until the end is approximately ¾in (2 cm) long.

Take a bobbin which has broken off in one hand and the end of the thread in the other. Wrap the thread around two fingers, (still holding the end), (diagram 6A). Make a loop, by putting the thread between the loop and the end and, placing it through the loop around the fingers, (diagram 6B). Make the weaver's knot by gently pulling this loop without allowing the end to pass through it, do not pull the knot too tight, (diagram 6C).

The broken end is now put through this loop, (diagram 6D), and the bobbin and the end of the thread from the weaver's knot are now pulled in opposite directions to tighten it and secure the broken thread. Test the knot by gently pulling the bobbin to see if it has held properly. It is sometimes necessary to repeat this if it has not done so.

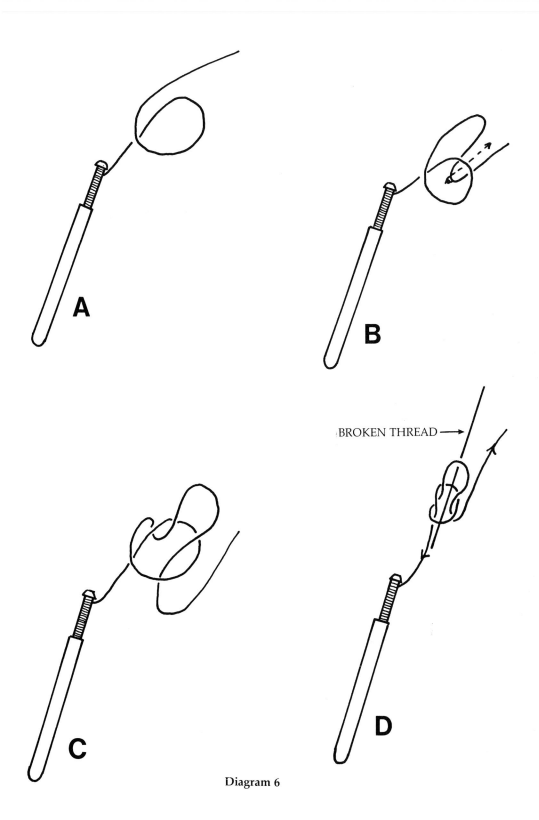

BROKEN THREAD →

A

B

C

D

Diagram 6

How to get rid of knots.

Should a thread break or knot appear because it has not been wound sufficiently on to the bobbin before commencing, there are several ways of removing them. If it is a *downright thread* in *whole stitch*, it can be looped around a pin and the resultant loop cut when this section of the work has been completed and finished off.

If it is a *downright thread in half stitch* the work must be unpicked until the knot is at the edge of the work when it can be crossed (cross = left over right) with the downright bobbin beside the coarse thread. Continue working until this thread has been in this position for ½in (7 mm), then remove this bobbin by making two whole stitches instead of the usual one at the end of the row and remove a pair in the usual way by tying the two bobbins (one of these will be the knotted one), inside the coarse thread and tying them three times before cutting them off. It will now be necessary to add a new pair to replace this pair.

If there is *a knot in the runners* wait until it is one of a pair to work a row. Ensure the knotted bobbin is not the leading one of the pair and make the first whole stitch of the row and cross the knotted bobbin with the downright one beside the coarse thread. It must remain in the work for ½in (12 mm) before being replaced by a new pair.

INDICATION OF PATTERN MARKINGS

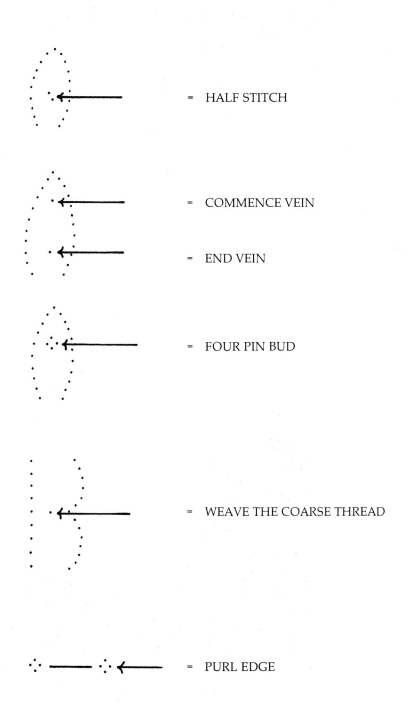

= HALF STITCH

= COMMENCE VEIN

= END VEIN

= FOUR PIN BUD

= WEAVE THE COARSE THREAD

= PURL EDGE

PRICKING ONE

PATTERN 1 (120 thread)

Whole Stitch Leaf

Start at the top of the main central leaf. Put a pin in the top hole and angle it slanting towards the back of the pillow (not vertical) to keep the threads close to the pillow and not rising up the pin. Hang four pairs of bobbins on this pin with the knotted one of each pair on the left. (fig 7) Hang on two more pairs with the bobbin without knots on the left and the two with knots between the other four pairs. (fig 8) *Place the coarse pair* under the downright (knotted) bobbin and over the runners (unknotted bobbins) and leave at the back of the pillow. (fig 9) Twist all the other pairs twice (right over left). Start the first row on the right hand side. Make a whole stitch and twist both pairs three times. Take the left hand of the two pairs to the left in whole stitch to within the last pair, twist the runners working the row three times and *put the pin under them sloping it slightly outwards and*

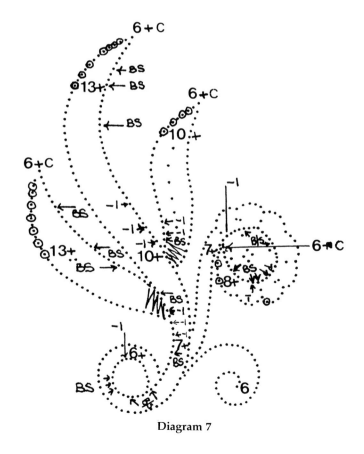

Diagram 7

backwards. (all pins must slope thus to stop the threads rising up the pins).
Make a whole stitch with the remaining pair and twist both pairs three
times. *Bring down the coarse thread* (fig 10) inside two pairs on the left hand
side and one pair on the right hand side. As the pattern widens it will be
necessary to add pairs of bobbins. For this, first pattern the holes where
these additional pairs are needed is indicated on the diagram. *To add a pair
in whole stitch.* (Pairs are added on the outside of a curve). Work to the side
where the extra pair is needed- twist three times and put in a pin. The new
pair are put under this pair of runners which have made the last row (fig
11) and then are put around the pin from outside to inside and *inside* the
coarse thread. (fig 12) Lastly the edge whole stitch is made and both pairs
are twisted three times. At the widest part of the leaf thirteen pairs plus a
coarse pair will be needed.

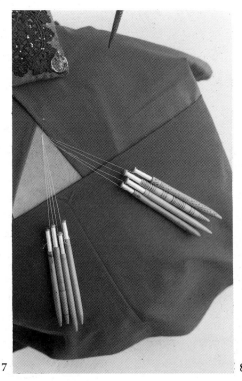

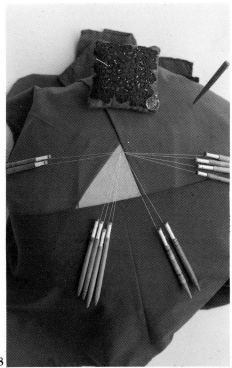

7

8

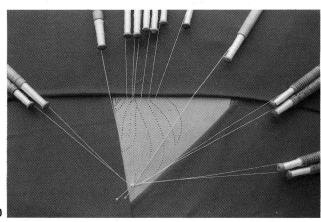

10

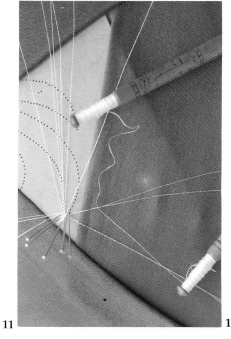

11

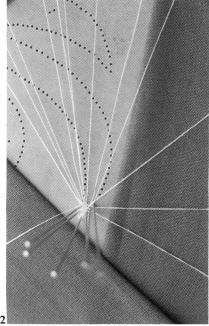

12

Back Stitches

At intervals on the right hand side (the inside of the curve) it will be necessary to use some of the holes twice. On this first pattern the holes are marked 'B/S'. On reaching one of these holes twist the runners *once* only, put in a pin but do not make an edge stitch. (fig 14) Work the same runners back in whole stitch as usual and then work a second row towards the back stitch. On reaching this hole remove the last pin, and replace it in the same hole (ignoring the little loop from the first time you used the pin). Make an edge stitch and twist both pairs three times. (fig 15)

13

N.B. When working the next edge stitch on the opposite isde to the back stitch be *very* careful not to pull the edge pair of runners too much as they are the ones which made the first row of the back stitch and are now unsupported by a pin and will pull the coarse thread away from the edge.

Taking Out Pairs in Whole Stitch

This is carried out on the inside of a curve. (In the first pattern the holes where this is necessary are marked -1). Work the edge stitch at this pin then take the two bobbins inside the coarse thread and lay them to the back of the pillow (fig 13). Work a row before cutting off these bobbins close to the work. (In working this row before cutting off the bobbins the ends of thread cannot work through to the other side, which when finished, is the right side of the lace).

The final circular part of the base of this first leaf is worked using seven pairs and a coarse pair until half way around when one more pair is removed.

After putting in the last pin work one more row. All but the coarse pair are now 'sewn' into the side of the leaf to finish.

Lay the coarse pair to the back of the pillow.

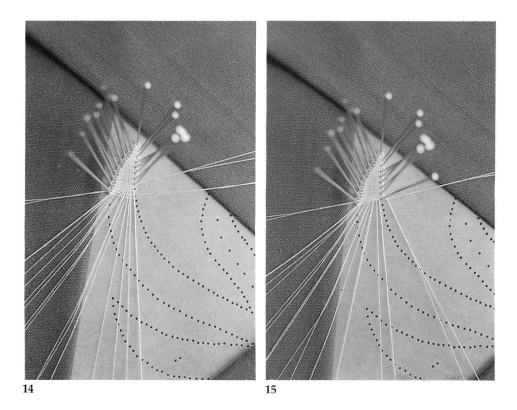

14   15

Sewing

Start sewing from the side where you have the one pair of runners. (Because the pair used to work the last row will now be sewn last of all and the work remains flexible to the last pair).

There are two types of sewings. Those into the front of the pin hole - flat sewings, and those into the side bars - raised sewings. Mostly the latter are more useful and look better.

When all the pairs have been sewn and tied three times put the pins back into the holes. Make a bunch with the threads by lifting all but the last pair in each side, cross these under the others. Tie one bobbin from each side over the others three times, and then the second one from each side over the others three times. (If there are seven or more pairs of bobbins then it is better to make two or more bunches depending on the number sewn). Cut off the coarse pair close to the lace, and also the bunches.

How to Make a FLAT Sewing
Put the needlepin into the hole where the pin was and out under the front edge, place one thread of the pair under the needlepin and bring it through the edge - keep this loop on the needlpin - and place the other bobbin of the pair through this. (fig 17) Remove the needlepin and gently pull the pairs and tie them both three times. (Right over left, left over right, right over left).

How to Make a RAISED Sewing
This is worked in the same way but by putting the needle pin into the pinhole and under one of the side bars. (fig 16)

This method makes it possible to sew two pairs per hole - one into each side bar. Raised sewings are usually easier to work and give the better appearance.

16

17

Whole Stitch Leaf with Twisted Vein

This is a whole stitch leaf with a twisted vein. It is started with six pairs plus a coarse pair, in exactly the same way as the first leaf. Only four pairs are added this time however (10 pairs and a coarse pair) as the vein helps to fill the leaf. Add pairs at the holes indicated and back stitch as before where necessary. (To keep the lace at right angle to the pin line).

Three Twisted Vein

When all the pairs have been added, start the vein. When the edge stitch has been made and the pairs twisted three times whole stitch through four pairs. (To the centre of the downright pairs). On the first row twist the runners once - work to the other side and back to the centre of the downright pairs, twist the runners twice and finish the row. Work back to the centre and on this and subsequent rows twist the runners three times. (fig 18) Close the vein at the last center hole in the leaf by twisting twice, then on the next row once and after that not at all Reduce to seven pairs plus a coarse pair near the bottom of the leaf. Work the last pinhole and then one more row before sewing out. Put the coarse threads to the back of the pillow. Sew out and tie three times the seven remaining pairs starting again from the side where there is one pair of runners.

Replace pins. Make two bunches (one of four pairs, one of three pairs) and cut off the close to the lace. Cut off the coarse threads.

Half Stitch Leaf

Start as the other two leaves with six pairs plus a coarse pair. The first row is worked in whole stitch. After the first pin has been put in, the edge stitch made, and both pairs twisted three times the subsequent rows are in half stitch. (fig 19) Remember the *first* and *last* stitch of the row with the coarse thread is whole stitch. (Add pairs and back stitch where indicated). Thirteen pairs and a coarse pair will be needed at the widest part.

18

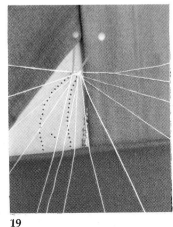

19

31

Adding Pairs in Half Stitch

Work to the pin where a new pair is needed, twist three times and put in the pin. Add as before, under this pair of runners and around the pin from outside to inside; place inside the coarse thread. Because when making half stitch all the pairs except the first and last downright pair are twisted right over left it is necessary to twist the pairs as in diagram 8. As the leaf narrows it will be necessary to take out pairs.

Taking Out Pairs in Half Stitch

This is slightly different to taking out pairs in whole stitch. *Two whole stitches are made* at the beginning or end of the row on the side where a pair is to be taken out. Make the edge stitch and before working another row, take the pair of bobbins inside the coarse thread, *tie them three times* and cut them off. (They can be left at the back of the pillow while the next row is worked and then cut off to avoid the ends working through to the front of the lace).

Where the half stitch leaf joins the first whole stitch leaf on the right hand side, work as in diagram 7.

After the last hole on the right work to the left and back again to the right hand side, where you now have no holes in which to put a pin. Sew in the edge pair of runners left from the previous row into the top bar of the adjacent hole in the whole stitch leaf. Tie three times and cut off.

The runners which have made the last row sew into the same hole, but the bottom bar, tie once and use them again for the next row. (These are *not* twisted either before or after the sewing).

Cut out the one coarse thread and the downright beside it, on the right hand side.

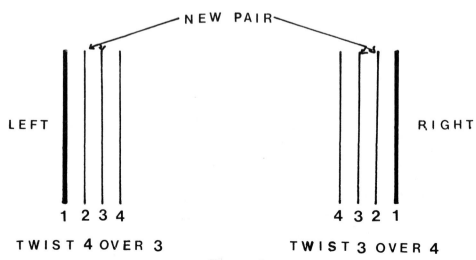

ADDING PAIRS IN HALF STITCH

NEW PAIR

LEFT

RIGHT

1 2 3 4

4 3 2 1

TWIST 4 OVER 3

TWIST 3 OVER 4

Diagram 8

Use the last hole on the left, work one more row in whole stitch (fig 20). Sew in the runners which have just made the last row and tie them. Throw back the coarse threads as these are never sewn. Sew in the other pair of runners and the remaining downright pairs, replace the pins, (fig 21) tie them all three times and make two bunches. (fig 22)

20

21

22

The Flower

Start with six pairs as before and when they are hung on the pin, but before they are twisted, add a *magic thread*. This is a piece of the fine lace cotton about 18in (45 cms) long. Fold it in half and put it under half the bobbins as shown in fig 23. This is used later when sewing into this hole. (All that is required is to place one of the bobbins being sewn into the looped end of the thread, pull the cut ends and this will pull the thread of the bobbin through. *Carefully* remove the magic thread and put the other runner of the pair through the loop). (fig 24) If this magic thread is not used the sewing must be made with *the pin still in the hole,* as if it is removed all the loops where the bobbins have been hung on the pin make a sewing impossible.

Twist all the pairs twice and add the coarse pair as before.

The first section of the flower is worked in whole stitch. Increase where indicated to eight pairs plus the coarse pair, take out one pair and back stitch where indicated as the scallop narrows.

Weave the coarse thread between each division as follows.

Finish with the edge stitch having been made on the *innermost* hole of the scallop. Take the coarse thread on this side and weave it over and under all the downright pairs, then over and under the other coarse thread on the inside of the flower and again over and under all the downright pairs finishing where it commenced (to the right of the two pairs of runners). fig 25

Work the first whole stitch of the row and tie the runners once to keep the coarse thread up in place - now change to half stitch making a whole stitch with the coarse pair at the end of the row as usual.

Add one pair at the second hole on the outside edge.

Work all the scallops in this way with alternate whole and half stitch.

After the last scallop weave the coarse pair through and continue down the stem in whole stitch with seven pairs plus a coarse pair. On reaching the pin where the flower was started, join to it by using the magic thread as previously described. Join to the central leaf stem in the same way as for the half stitch leaf. Take out pairs where indicated and sew out remaining pairs - tie three times and bunch. Cut off these and the coarse pair.

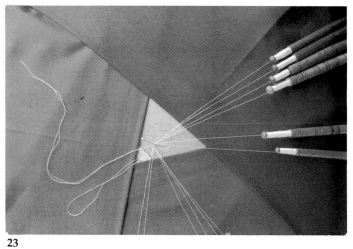

23

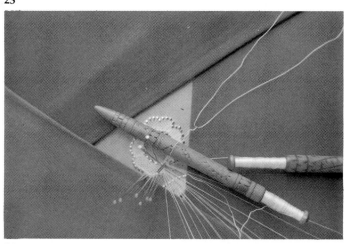

24

25

Ribbed Tendril.

Hang six pairs on the pin at the top of the tendril. (No coarse pair is needed). Twist them all twice. The pinhole edge is always on the *outside of the curve* and the plain side on the inside.

Take the left-hand two pairs, make a whole stitch and twist both pairs three times. Whole stitch the right-hand pair through all the pairs to the right, twist them once and leave them, (fig 26). take the downright pair to the left of this pair and whole stitch to the left through all but the last pair, twist three times, (fig 27), put in a pin and make an edge stitch. (Whole stitch with both runners and twist them both three times). Take the left-hand pair of runners to work the next row, work in whole stitch to the end (including the twisted pair left from the last row), twist the runners once and leave them (fig 28). Repeat as before. Having come to the last hole, work one more row. (One pair of runners are now on each side of the downright pairs). Sew both of these in and tie them three times. Sew any of the downright pairs possible and then bunch in the usual way.

26

27

28

HOW TO MAKE A LEADWORK

A leadwork is made with two pairs of bobbins. Lengthen the second from the left and use this as the weaver. The remaining three pairs should be fairly short *Keeping the weaver very slack take it over the centre of the three bobbins, under and over the righthand one and under the centre one, then over and under the lefthand bobbin. (The weaver is now second from the left which is where it started). Gently pull up the weaver, holding the three bobbins are spreading them to govern the width of the leadwork*. Repeat * to * until the leadwork is the desired length. At no point must the weaver be allowed to pull tight or the leadwork will be spoilt. If it should be pulled just a little too much, spread the outer two bobbins of the three to widen the leadwork. If however, it has pulled very narrow then the leadwork must be undone and started again.

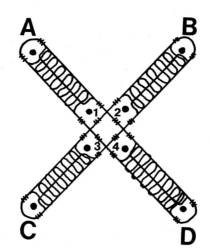

Diagram 9

DIAMOND FILLING

This is the filling used in the centre of the flower. Sew in two pairs of bobbins above holes A and B (diagram 9). With each of the two pairs make a whole stitch, twist three times and put a pin between the pairs. Lengthen the second bobbin from the left and use as the weaver for the leadwork (fig 29) which must reach as far as hole 1. Twist both pairs three times and put pin 1 between them. Tuck the weaver into the cover cloth to prevent pulling the thread and spoiling the leadwork, (fig 30). Repeat this with the two pairs at B to hole 2.

With the two centre pairs make a whole stitch and three twists. (No pin)

Make a whole stitch and three twists with the two left hand pairs and put a pin between them in hole 3. Make a whole stitch and three twists with the two pairs on the right and put pin 4 between them. Take the two centre pairs make a whole stitch and three twists. (No pin)

38

Make a leadwork with the two left hand pairs to hole C. Twist them both three times, put pin C between them, make a whole stitch, sew out both pairs, tie them three times (fig 31) and cut off the bobbins.

Repeat this with the two right hand pairs working the leadwork to hole D.

Carefully remove all the pins one by one and turn the lace over.

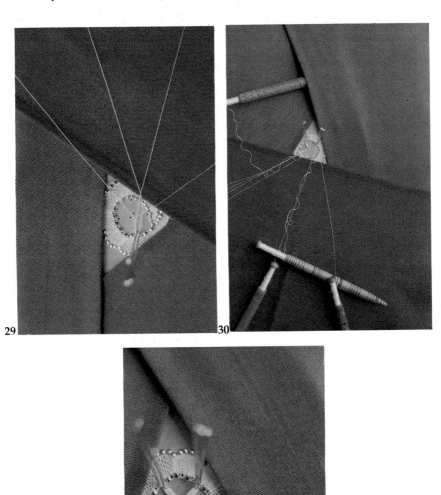

29   30

31

PRICKING TWO

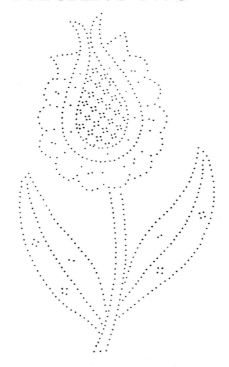

PATTERN 2 (120 thread)

Start with a pin at point A. (Diagram 10) hang on six pairs of bobbins, four unknotted ones to the right and two on the left, twist all the pairs twice. Put the coarse pair under the downright pairs and over the runners and leave at the back of the pillow until the first whole stitch row is worked. Start on the right hand side - make a whole stitch and twist both pairs three times. Take the left hand pair of the two and work to the left through all but the last pair, twist three times and put up the pin. Make a whole stitch with the end pair and twist both pairs three times. bring down the coarse thread on the left, between the pins and inside both pairs of twisted runners, the right hand coarse thread comes down on the right inside the twisted pair of runners at the edge. Continue in whole stitch, back stitching where indicated on the daigram to keep the lace at right angles to the pins.

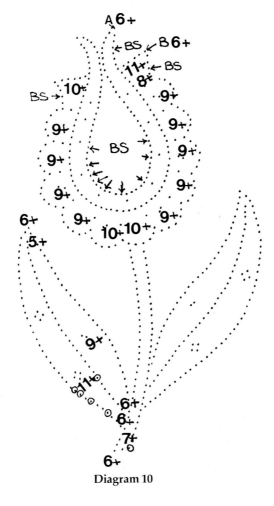

Diagram 10

41

Where the holes start in the centre of the whole stitch commence the *vein*. This is worked in the same way as the vein in pattern 1. (Twist the runners once in the centre of the downrights on the next row, twice on the one after that on the next and subsequent rows three times. Finish the vein by doing the reverse, two and one twist. Soon after closing the vein *the braids almost touch and it is necessary to attach them one to the other.* To do this make the edge stitch but do not twist the runners. Sew in the nearest pair to the complete lace and tie them once, (fig 32) make a second whole stitch with both pairs of runners and twist them both three times. This will be necessary for the five holes which almost touch. Continue backstitching where necessary.

32

Finishing at a point.   Three holes from the point lay out a pair from inside the coarse thread on the right hand side. (DO NOT CUT THEM OFF). Work to the other side and back again to the right and again lay back a pair from the same side. Work the last pinhole.

Put the coarse pair to the back of the pillow. Work one whole stitch row through *all* the pairs (including the edge runners), tie the pair that have worked the row three times. Tie the two pairs of downrights three times. make a bunch with the five pairs by crossing the extreme edge pair on each side under the runners and tie one bobbin from each side three times over the top of the other two pairs and then repeat with the other pair. (fig 33) Push down all the pins except the last two at the point. Cut off the coarse threads close to the lace. Open out the pairs layed back, one bobbin from each pair on opposite sides of the pillow. Bring the bunch between the two pins and twist them a little to make a cord and lay them between the opened out pairs.(fig 34) Tie each of these pairs over the cord thus securing it over the back of the lace. (fig 35) Cut off all the bobbins as close as possible, but without cutting off the knots tying the bunch!

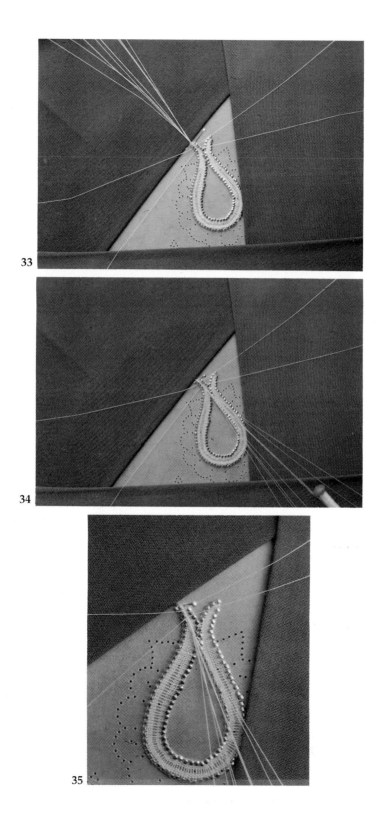

33

34

35

Straight Start. Diagram 11 Start at B. Put in a pin and hang on six pairs and a coarse pair in the same way as the previous section, work the first row pin 2 and bring down the coarse pair. Work to the right through two pairs and leave the runners. Take the downright pair to their left as the runners for the next row and whole stitch through the pair to their left, twist three times and put up a pin at 3. Add one pair and put them inside the coarse thread, and then add a second pair to the left of these, also inside the coarse thread. Make up the edge stitch and twist both pairs three times. Again whole stitch through two pairs to the right and leave the runners. Take the pair of downrights to their left of the whole stitch left to the next pin 4, add two more pairs as before. Make the edge stitch and twist three times, work to the right through two pairs. Take the pair of downrights to the left of the runners and whole stitch left to the next pin 5, add one pair. Make the edge stitch and whole stitch through two pairs, leave the runners and again whole stitch to the left. This time the runners which work the row top sew in and tie once. (There are now elevan pairs and a coarse pair). The edge pair on the left are no longer needed as sewings will now be made on this side. Sew in the edge pair and tie them three times and cut off. Take the pair of runners which worked the last row (and were sewn in and tied once at the end of the last row) and whole stitch them to the right. Make the usual edge stitch and take out one pair from inside the coarse thread on the right hand side before the next row. Reduce to nine pairs and a coarse pair by the time the end of this section is reached. Use top, (or raised) sewing for this on the left hand side which gives the edge a slightly 'raised' appearance, on the right side of the lace. When a back stitch is needed on this side sew into the top and bottom bars of a pinhole to use the hole twice. Otherwise always sew into the bottom bar. Sew with the bottom thread of the pair and put the top one down through the loop. Tie the runners once after the sewing to keep good tension. (When pairs are sewn in as mentioned, the threads stay side-by-side and do not twist one over the other).

When backstitching on hole four on the right hand side of this section and *using the pin for the first time angle the pin towards the lace* instead of away from it as usual. As there is a sewing on the opposite side it is impossible to pull the first loop of the back stitch. However, by putting the pin in at this angle it minimises the size of the loop which is not visible when the hole has been used for the second time.

Take out one more pair on the left hand side (eight plus the coarse pair) before weaving the coarse thread through the downrights as in the first pattern. Remember this always weaves from the outside to the inside of the scallop and back again to follow the curve of the scallop. Alternate sections of this pattern are in half stitch. N.B. Keep all the bobbins on the left well over to the left *do not* pull the pairs away or a space will appear between this section and the previous one already made.

Use the number of pairs indicated for each section; adding a pair on the outside just *before* the scallop reaches its widest part and taking out a pair just *after* it narrows. Carry on to the last whole stitch section finishing at the bottom with ten pairs and a coarse pair.

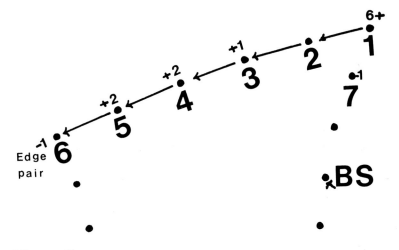

Diagram 11

Straight Finish.   Diagram 12 After the last hole on the right work the first whole stitch and tie the runners once or the coarse thread will pull away from the corner pin, work through two more pairs, (three pairs in all), and leave the runners. Take the next downright pair to the right of these runners and whole stitch them through the two pairs to their right and make the usual edge stitch. Before working the next row, take out the pair inside the coarse thread and lay them at the back of the pillow.

(N.B.   If this had been a *half stitch* section this straight finish would still be made in whole stitch but the pairs taken out would have to be *tied three times*).

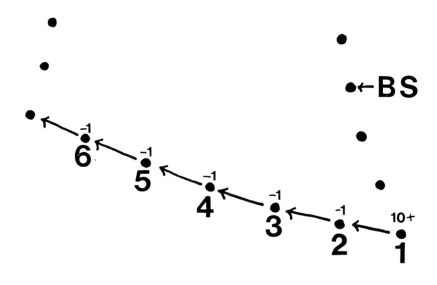

Diagram 12

Work again to the left through three pairs and leave the runners, take the pair of downrights to the right of these and work to the right, put in a pin and make an edge stitch. Take the pair inside the coarse thread and lay to the back of the pillow..

Work * to * until the last hole has been worked. Five pairs will have been laid out at the back of the pillow leaving two runners, three downright pairs and two coarse threads. Take the pair of downrights on the right of the left hand coarse thread and lay them to the back of the pillow with the other five pairs.

Whole stitch to the left for the last row. Lay back the coarse threads. Sew the remaining four pairs and bunch them as before and cut off all the bobbins together with those put to the back of the pillow. (fig 36)

36.

Tip. To sew two runners into one side bar:- sew in one pair and tie them, then put them to the back of the pillow and it is possible to sew another pair into the same bar.

Stem. Hang six pairs and a coarse pair on the corner pin. Four pairs with the unknotted bobbins on the right and then two pairs with the unknotted bobbins on the left in the usual way. The coarse pair goes under the six knotted bobbins now in the centre of the pillow, and over the six unknotted ones (the runners). Twist all the pairs twice (except the coarse pair) and work the first whole stitch row from right to left. Put in the pin and make the edge stitch. Bring down the coarse threads inside the one pair on the right and between the pins and inside the two pairs on the left. When working the next pin (the corner one), on the left add one more pair. After the first stitch of the next row on this side tie the runners once to keep the coarse thread out against the pin. Work with these seven pairs and the coarse pair to the top of the stem backstitching where necessary. Work one row after putting in the last pin. Sew out all the pairs except the coarse pair which are cut off close to the work. Sew from the side which has the one pair of runners towards the side which has the two pairs. (It will not matter if this is done the opposite way but this way it is easier as the last pair to be sewn is the last pair which worked a row. This means that the work is more flexible. If the other pair were sewn first then the work would be very taught while doing the rest of the sewing). When the sewings are complete and the pairs all tied three times, replace the pins in the holes and put the bobbins just sewn back in order between the pins. If the bunch is then made back over the stem (fig 37) the pinholes will remain distinct and look

37

much neater on the other side. This is always the best way to sew out when, as sometimes happens, whole stitch is sewn out into a half stitch section.

Right Hand Leaf.   Where possible it is always better to work up the whole stitch side of a *divided leaf* and back the half stitch side. When sewing whole stitch into half stitch there is a tendency unless worked very carefully for there to be a slight space between the two sections. With half stitch being an open stitch the reverse does not have this effect. *Pairs for this leaf are sewn into the stem* of the flower. This is done in the usual way but the pairs are *not* tied after sewing them in. Sew two pairs into each of the three holes in the stem on the whole stitch leaf side. Replace the pins in the holes when the pairs have been sewn in, this prevents the holes being pulled when the work commences. *Lift up a pin on the far side of the stem and hang the coarse pair on this one.* Place it between the pins of the sewn pairs inside two pairs of bobbins on the left and one pair on the right. (fig 38) (The loop which results from this cut off when the leaf is finished). The pair on the extreme right must now be twisted three times. Work the first row by making a whole stitch and three twists with the far left hand two pairs. Work up the leaf in whole stitch and add pairs as the work widens having increased to eleven pairs and a coarse pair when reaching the group of four holes in the centre of the leaf section.   This is called a four pin bud, and was worked right to left.

38

To work the *four pin bud* the whole stitch must be just above the top hole of the four. Whole stitch through six pairs (three downright plus three centre downright pairs leaving three downright pairs unworked), (fig 39) leave the runners and take the pair to their right and whole stitch them through two pairs to the right (fig 40).

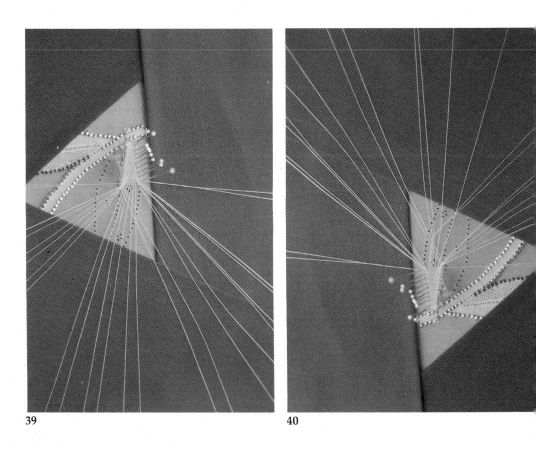

39   40

Take the two pairs to their left, (referred to hereafter as the two centre pairs) twist them three times and put a pin between them in the top hole of the four holes. (fig 41) Enclose this pin with a whole stitch and three twists. (fig 42) (It is a good idea to place a pin on either side of these two pairs to prevent taking the wrong pair as runners when working out on each side.)

Take the pair to the left of these pairs and work them out to the edge and back again to the centre, twist three times and put a pin under the pair into the left hand of the two holes.

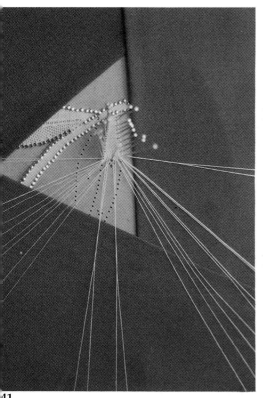

41

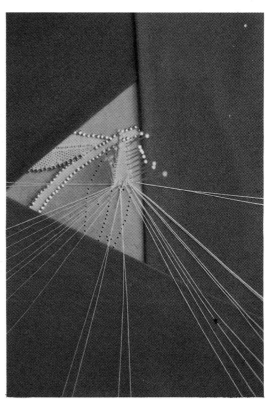

42

Take the left hand of the two pairs between the pins and make a whole stitch and three twists with them. replace the right hand of the two pairs inside the two pins. Take the pair to the right of the two pins and whole stitch them to the edge and back to the centre. Twist them three times and put a pin under them into the right hand of the two holes. Take the right hand pair inside the pins and with these two pairs make a whole stitch and three twists. (fig 43) (Replace the left hand of the two pairs inside the two pins). The runners on either side of the two pins now work out to their respective sides and back again to the centre. Leave them both here, untwisted. Remove the two pins and with the two pairs which were inside them (the two centre pairs) make a whole stitch and three twists and put a pin between them in the bottom hole. (fig 44) It is now possible to choose

 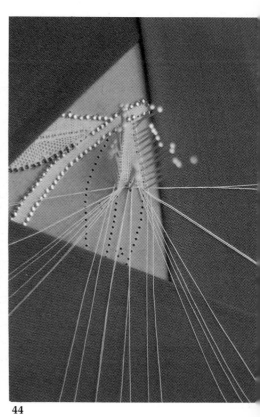

43   44

which way to work. This four pin bud was finished in the same direction it was started, to the right. (This is decided by working to the side which has most holes left to be used.) Before doing this the runners left on the right of the two centre pairs must be worked through the two centre pairs and the pair of runners to their left. (fig 45) These runners remain here to become downrights and the last pair worked through are then worked to the right to comlete the row. (fig 46)

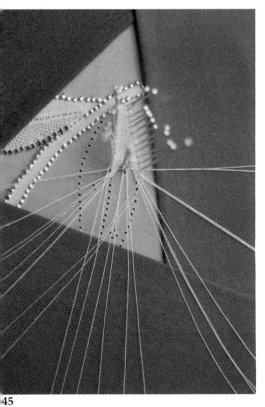

45

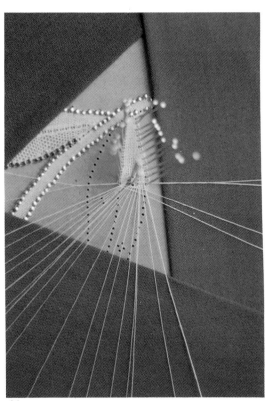

46

53

One of the things which make four pin buds look attractive is when all the threads come tightly around the four holes. This means that it must be started just above the top hole and finished close against the bottom one. This can sometimes mean that a back stitch has to be made on one side or the other. After the four pin bud has been completed it is important to keep easing the downright bobbins on either side of the side pins towards them so that a gap does not appear at the side.

Work the second four pin bud in the same way. After this has been made and the lace starts to narrow it will be necessary to take out some pairs on the right hand side. Reduce to six pairs plus the coarse pair at the tip of the leaf. *To work around the corner* it will be necessary to back stitch about three times into the top hole of the centre of the leaf. After the edge stitch *at the top point make the first stitch of the row and tie the runners once or they will pull away from the top pin hole.*

Make up the back stitch when the top of the leaf has been turned. Before working the next row take out one pair from the left hand side of the work. Change to half stitch now for the remainder of the leaf. The edge pair on the left of the work are no longer needed as sewings will now be made on this side. Untwist them and weave the coarse thread on this side over and under through them so that it lies on the extreme left of the work. Continue in half stitch remembering that the first and last stitch of the row is a whole stitch. When making the sewings on the left hand side work through to the end of the row *do not twist* but sew into the bottom bar of the pinhole, tie the runners once and continue. As before when needing to use a hole twice sew into the top and bottom bars. Increase as the leaf widens and at the widest point have nine pairs plus a coarse pair. Decrease as it narrow and finish this half stitch section with six pairs and a coarse pair. After the last pin, work one row in whole stitch. Throw back the coarse pair and sew in the other six pairs, tie them all three times and bunch them as before. Leave the ends of the bunch over the whole stitch stem. Cut off all pairs including the coarse pair.

Left Hand Leaf. This leaf is worked in the same way as the first one. At the bottom of the half stitch section however it is easier to work down to a point to finish. Where the leaf touches the stem the edge pair of runners which will no longer be needed to make edge stitches will be sewn out and tied three times and cut off. Sewings will now be made at each hole on this side. After two holes the coarse thread and the downright bobbin beside it can be cut out. Continue on and descrease down to the end with four pairs a coarse thread and one odd one.

Work the last row as a whole stitch row. Cut off the coarse thread and sew out all the other pairs. There will be one odd bobbin, when making the last sewing and before tying the pair put this odd bobbin in between the two and tie three times over it. Put in the pins where the sewings have been made, make a bunch and cut off the bobbins.

Four pin filling was used for the flower centre.
N.B. When the filling has been completed leave the pins in for one or two days to allow the filling to set.

TO MAKE A TEMPLATE AND PRICK A FILLING

All Honiton lace fillings are made using 1mm graph paper. In order to prick a filling it is necessary to make a template.

For this a sheet of 1mm graph paper, a technical drawing (or similar), pen will be needed, also a pricking board, pricker and either exposed, cleaned X-ray film or thick acetate sheet, (fig 47).

Refer to the line diagrams at the back of the book for the spacing of the dots. Using the pen, dot an area of about 2in (5 cm) (fig 48). Take great care when doing this as accuracy is essential. When this is completed place the graph paper on the pricking board and on top of this the film or acetate, pin down and *very* carefully prick holes where the dots appear on the graph paper, (fig 49).

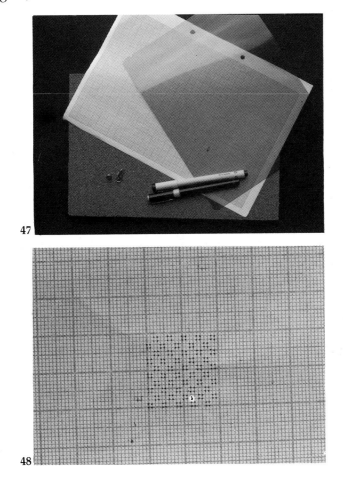

47

48

49

50

Unpin the film and position it over the space to be filled in the pattern. Align it so that the blocks are vetically and horizontally straight and with as many complete blocks as possible. Pin down securely and *carefully* prick through the holes in the film (fig 50) on to the pattern beneath. When all the holes have been pricked remove the film and sew in the bobbins for the filling. (The instructions for this are at the back of the book).

When only part of a block is possible cover over the missing holes on the line diagram and follow the direction of the lines visible to know how to make the part of the filling necessary.

N.B. These film or acetate sheets can be used many times if used with great care. Tracing graph paper can be used instead but it is not as transparent so more difficult to position correctly and also tears easily.

PRICKING THREE

PATTERN 3 (120 Thread)

1. Start at the outside edge of the central ring. (diagram 14) Hang six pairs on a pin. (Four unknotted pairs on the right and two unknotted pairs on the left with all the bobbins with knots in the centre). Put in a magic thread, by folding a length of fine thread in half and putting it under half of these bobbins. Put it to the back of the pillow for use later.

   Twist all the bobbins twice, Put the coarse thread under the downright pairs and over the two pairs of runners on the right and one pair on the left. Start on the right hand side with a whole stitch and twist both pairs three times. Take the left hand pair in whole stitch through all but the last pair on the left. Twist the runners which have just made the row three times and put pin (2) under them. make a whole stitch and twist three times with the last pair on the left. Bring down the coarse thread on the left between the two pins and inside these two pairs on the left and inside the one pair of runners on the right. Work to the right in whole stitch through two pairs, leave the

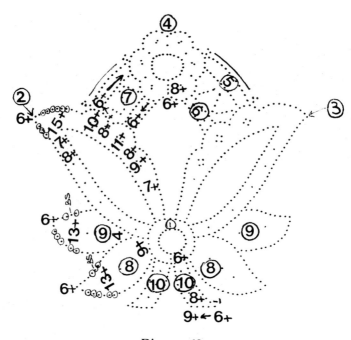

Diagram 13

58

runners and take the downright pair to their left in whole stitch, left to the next hole. (3) Twist three times put in a pin, make a whole stitch and twist both pairs three times. After the first stitch of the next row tie the runners once to keep the coarse thread against the corner pin. Continue in whole stitch, back stitching on the inside of the circle when necessary. After the last pinhole has been used work one more row. Sew in all the pairs, but not the coarse pair which are cut off close to the work. Tie all the pairs three times and replace the pins in the holes before making a bunch with them. Cut off all the bobbins but leave the ends long (about 4in) (10 cms)) this will make sewing near here again much easier and there will be no fear of pulling out these ends.

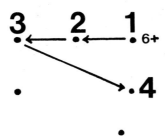

Diagram 14

2.   Start at the point of this shape with six pairs and a coarse pair. have four pairs with unknotted bobbins on the left and two on the right, as the first row will be worked from left to right (Towards the side with the most holes).

Back stitch on the left hand side and increase to fifteen pairs and a coarse pair by the time the top hole in the centre is reached. *The braid is now divided into two.*

There will now be two pairs of runners on the right and one pair on the left.

Divide the downright - put four and a half pairs (including one coarse thread) on the left and six and a half pairs (including the other coarse thread) on the right. This will leave four bobbins in the centre. Weave a new coarse pair through these and put it to the back of the pillow. (fig 51)

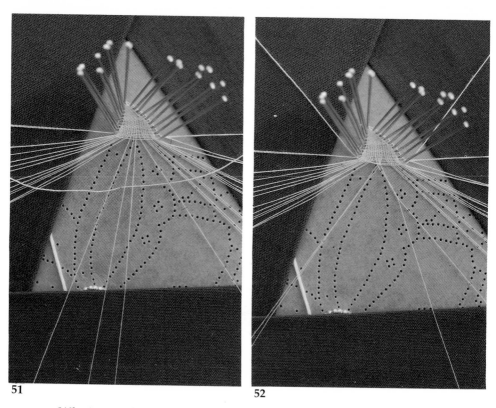

51   52

Whole stitch these centre two pairs and twist them both three times. (fig 52)

Bring down the right hand of the new coarse pair to the right of the two centre twisted pairs. (fig 53) Work a row from the ouside right hand edge through the coarse thread and twist three times. (fig 54) Add a pair at this pin and put them to the back of the pillow. (fig 55) (This will become the extra pair of runners needed for the other section). Make an edge stitch with the right hand of the two twisted pairs. This has now completed the division on the right. (Nine pairs and a coarse pair). To complete the left hand side the coarse thread is brought down inside the remaining twisted centre pair. Bring down the new runners, put to the back of the pillow and use them to work to the left. On returning to the centre, the edge pair is the remaining twisted centre pair. There will now be seven pairs and a coarse pair in the left hand section. Add one more pair and then work a twisted vein in the centre of the braid by twisting the runners twice in the centre of each row, starting and finishing it where indicated on the pattern. After the last pin in this section work one more row. Cut off both coarse threads. Sew out all the pairs (two per pinhole) starting from the side where there is one pair of runners and tie them three times. Replace the four pins, lay the bobbins back through these and bunch them over the work just completed. (Make two small bunches rather than one large one). Leave long ends.

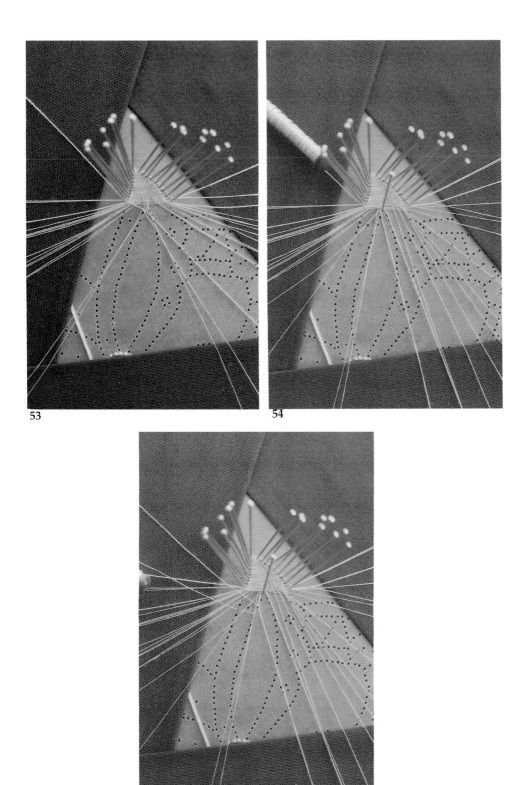

53

54

55

61

The other side with the four pin buds may now be continued. Add one more pair before making the first four pin bud. (Ten pairs plus a coarse pair). When dividing the downright pairs leave the extra pair on the right of the four pin bud, as this side is slightly wider. (Follow instructions in Pattern 2 for the four pin bud). After the four pin bud has been completed and before weaving the coarse thread through at the end of the scallop take out two pairs. As the next section widens increase by three pairs to eleven pairs plus a coarse pair.

Take these out again after the four pin bud and before weaving the coarse thread through.

Add one pair before making the last four pin bud. Reduce to seven pairs and a coarse pair for the remainder of this section. Work one more row after the last pin, cut off the coarse pair. Sew out all the pairs and tie them three times. Replace the pins where the sewings have been made, lift the sewn pairs back between them and make two bunches over the braid just worked.

3. Repeat as above for the matching shape on the other side of the design.

4. **Half Stitch Flower**
    Start at the outside edge of the flower by putting in a pin in hole 1. (diagram 15) Hang on four pairs with unknotted bobbins on the right and then two pairs with the unknotted bobbins on the left. (Magic thread). Fold a length of fine thread in half and put under half the bobbins and leave at the back of the pillow. Add a coarse pair under the downright pairs and over the runners and put at the back of the pillow. Twist all the pairs (not the coarse pair) twice. Start on the right and work to hole 2. Make the edge stitch and bring down the coarse thread inside these two pairs and inside the one pair of runners on the

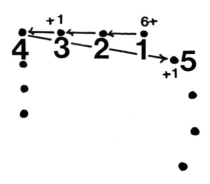

Diagram 15

right hand side. Whole stitch to the right through two pairs, leave the runners and work the pair to their left as runners to hole 3. Add a pair, make the edge stitch and again work through two pairs. Leave the runners and work the pair to their left to hole 4. Make an edge stitch, twist both pairs three times, and make a whole stitch with the coarse. Tie the runners once now before changing to half stitch to prevent the threads pulling away from the corner hole. Work to hole 5 and add one more pair. (there are now eight pairs and a coarse pair).Work the flower back stitching on the inside edge as necessary and weaving the coarse thread between the petals always from the outside to the inside and back again. After the last pin work one whole stitch row. Cut off the coarse pair and sew in the other pairs two pairs per hole. (Use the magic thread, as in Pattern 1, on the flower). Make two bunches after first replacing the four pins.

5. Sew in six pairs (two pairs per pinhole) for the purl edged braid at the top of the design. Lift up a pin at the back and hang a coarse thread on it. Place it inside two pairs on the left and one pair on the right. Twist the one pair on the right three times. (fig 56) Start working in whole stitch with the first two pairs on the left and twist both pairs three times. Take the inside pair and whole stitch to the right through the coarse thread. (fig 57) Twist three times.

 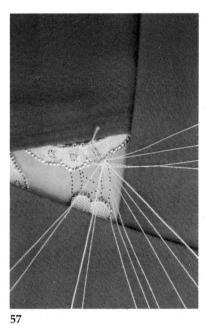

56   57

Working a Purl. (*Right* handed purl). With the pair which have just worked the rows and twisted three times, and the edge pair, make a whole stitch. (Pull up well before making the purl as it is not possible to do so afterwards.) Twist the right hand pair seven times, (fig 58). take a pin in the right hand and hold the far right hand bobbin in the left hand. Put the pin under this thread and bring the pin over towards you and place in the pinhole, (fig 59). Lay this bobbin down on the far right. Take the other one of the pair and place it around the same pin, from outside to inside and lay it second from the right, (fig 60). Twist this pair once right over left. Wiggle them gently to settle and tighten the purl. Make a whole stitch with this pair and the other runners to their left. Twist both pairs three times (fig 61) and work the next row.

Working a left handed purl. This is made in the same way but holding the bobbin in the right hand and the pin in the left when making the purl. The second thread goes around the pin from outside to inside and lies second from the left. Wiggle them, gently to settle and tighten the purl. This pair is now twisted *twice, left over right.* Pull up gently, make a whole stitch and twist both pairs three times.
N.B. (It is usually possible to choose, by the direction of working, which side the purls will be worked. A right handed person usually finds right handed purls easier to work and a left handed person, left handed purls.)

Work to the end of this section, lay back the coarse pair, sew out all the pairs and tie them three times, replace the pins and bunch the pairs back over the braid.

6. Six pairs and a coarse pair are needed for the next section which is made in the same way as the previous one but omitting the purls and working a two twist vein in the centre. These two sections are repeated the far side of the flower.

7. **Purl Pin Bars**
Sew in four pairs of bobbins in the first hole of the section marked 'X'
With the right hand of the four pairs work in whole stitch through the three pairs on the left. Twist this pair once and leave them. *Take the pair to their right in whole stitch through the other two pairs to their right. Make a purl by twisting this pair seven times. Take the far right hand bobbin and put a pin under this thread and over the top towards you and into the pinhole. Take the bobbin to its left (the other one of this pair) and put it around the pin from outside to inside and inside the first bobbin, twist this pair once, whole stitch them through the other three, twist once, and leave.* Continue * to * until the last purl is made, work in whole stitch to the left and sew this pair into the hole in line with the purl bar. Tie them once and then whole stitch them through one pair. Sew this pair into the edge and tie once. Turn the pillow and work the next bar in the same way. After the last purl in this section work in whole stitch through the three pairs, twist the runners once and leave them. Take the pair to their right and whole stitch through the two pairs on the right sew this pair into the edge and tie once. Work in whole stitch through one pair and sew this pair in to the edge, tie once and turn the pillow. (it will be noted that on this bar one more row has been worked). The last bar is now the same as the first. After the last purl work two whole stitch rows and sew out all four pairs. Tie them three times and cut them off.
This is repeated on the other side of the design.

8. These two whole stitch leaves have a *'Ladder Trail'*, (or *'Mittens'*) in the centre.
The leaves are started at the point with six pairs plus a coarse pair. (Four unknotted bobbins on the right and two on the left). Increase to thirteen pairs and a coarse pair. To start the *Ladder trail* work in whole

stitch through five pairs, (fig 62) twist the runners three times, leave them here, take the next pair of downrights to finish the row taking care to pull the first downrights you work through towards the centre of the leaf or a large gap will appear. (fig 63) Work from this side through five downright pairs and twist the runners three times. There should now be two pairs of twisted runners in the centre. (fig 64) make a whole stitch with these pairs and twist them both three times. (fig 65) Each pair now works out to the sides, an edge stitch is made and * the two pairs of runners work to the centre where they are twisted three times. They work a whole stitch together and are again twisted three times.* Continue in this manner until the second hole in the centre of the leaf where the Ladder Trail ends. To do this work to the centre as usual but *do not* twist the runners three times, (fig 66). N.B. When working keep pulling the centre downright pairs towards the centre. Do not allow the vein to become too large. One of the pairs is left as a downright pair and the other pair continue the row. Reduce to nine pairs plus a coarse pair at the bottom of the leaf. Cut off the coarse pair and sew out all the bobbins. Replace the pins in the holes, and lift the pairs carefully between them and lay them over the leaf and make two bunches. Cut off all the bobbins.

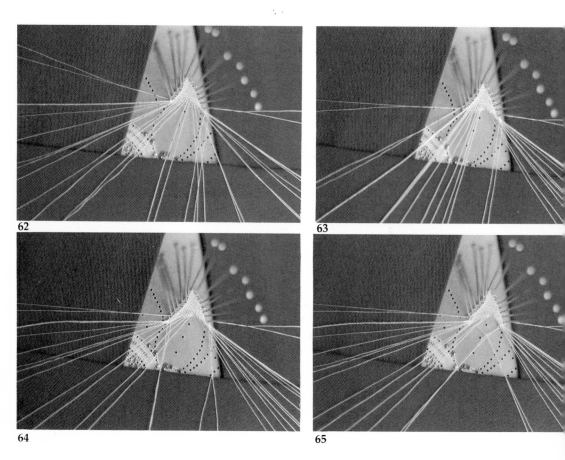

62

63

64

65

66

9. The two whole stitch leaves have *HALF STITCH VEINS* in the centre. Start with six pairs and a coarse pair in the same way as the previous two leaves. Increase to thirteen pairs and a coarse pair. This makes three pairs of runners and eleven dowright pairs.

Commence the half stitch vein by working five whole stitches. (fig 67). Twist the runners once and make a half stitch with the next pair, (fig 68), then continue the row with five whole stitches. When stopping this vein do not twist the runners or make the half stitch. N.B. All the time this vein is being worked it is important to pull the centre downright pairs towards the centre in order that the vein does not become too large. (fig 69). On reaching the last pinhole both edge pairs (one on each side of the leaf) will be sewn into the w ɔrk on either side, tied three times and cut off. The runners will work all the subsequent rows sewing in at each edge after the first stitch at the beginning of each of the next two rows tie the runners once to prevent the work pulling away from the edge. After sewing into the holes in this way the two coarse threads can be cut off. (Cutting them off too soon would leave a hole.) Work down to the point gradually reducing to four pairs. Sew these in, tie them three times, bunch them and cut them all off.

10. Start this right hand section by putting in a pin at the point nearest to leaf 8. Hang on six pairs and a coarse pair and work a straight start towards the opposite side No pairs are added at the second pin where the coarse pair are brought down into position.* Whole stitch to the right through two pairs, leave the runners and take the pair to their left, to the left to the next pinhole. Add a pair make the edge stitch* and repeat * to * twice more. Work in the same way to the last hole but do not add. (There are now nine pairs and a coarse pair). Work the edge stitch, then the first stitch of the row and tie the runners once before working the first complete row to the right hand side. After this next pin take out one pair on this side before working the next row. (Eight pairs and a coarse pair.) Use these pairs to finish this section.

Work one row after the last pin, sew out all the pairs, cut off the coarse pair, replace the pins, lift the pairs back between the pins and make two bunches over the work just completed. Cut off the bobbins.
The other similar shape is worked in the same way.

Fillings

The fillings used in the flower and sections two and three are Pin and a Stitch with leadworks. The flower has a group of four central leadworks and the other sections have two rows of Pin and a Stitch and two of leadworks.

This is more difficult to work and that is why Pin and a Stitch without leadworks is pricked in these spaces and is worked in the bottom circle of the design. Instructions for these are given at the back of the book in the 'filling' section.

The filling in the centre of the design is Fourpin Flower and Leadworks.

When the fillings are completed allow the pins to remain in for two or three days before removing them to allow the filling to set. Remove all the pins carefully one at a time on completion of the work.

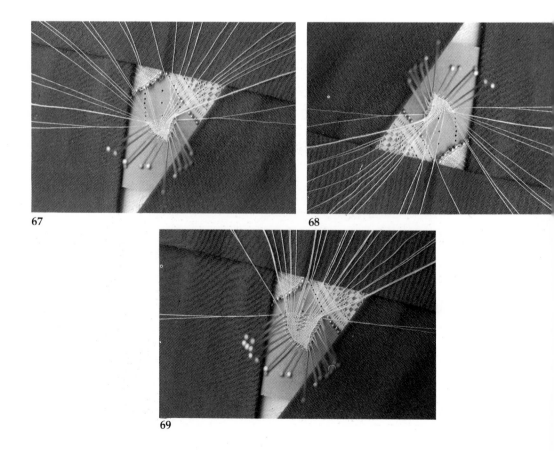

67

68

69

PRICKING FOUR

JAPANESE SAMPLER (170 thread)

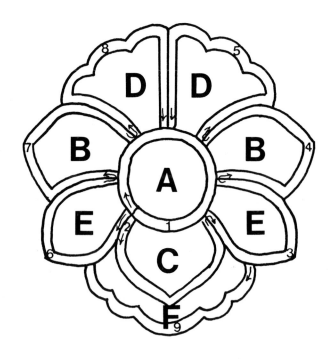

Diagram 16

Key to Filling Stitches

A Whole Stitch Block
B Toad in the Hole with Wide Leadworks
C Toad in the Hole
D Toad in the Hole with Enclosed Pins
E Toad in the Hole Variation
F Variation of Whole Stitch Block

The Central Whole Stitch Circle (1) Diagram 16

Hang seven pairs on a pin on the outer edge of the circle. (four unknotted bobbins on the right and three on the left). Put in a magic thread by folding a length of fine thread (about 12″ (30 cms) in half and place it under half the bobbins and leave at the back of the pillow. Twist all the pairs twice, right over left. Place the coarse thread under the downrights and over the two pairs of runners on the right and one pair on the left. Whole stitch to the hole on the left, make the edge stitch and bring down the coarse threads. The left hand one comes between the pins and inside the two pairs of runners on the left. The right hand one comes down inside the pair on the right. Work a straight start along the line of holes leading to the inner edge of the circle.

To do this * whole stitch to the right through two pairs and leave the runners. Take the downright pair to their left in whole stitch to the left through the remaining pair, put up the pin and add a pair. make the edge stitch * and repeat * to * once more but do not add a pair. When working the first row to the outside edge of the circle tie the runners once after the first stitch of the row as there is a right angle here and if this is not done a large pinhole will result, as the pairs will pull away from the corner. Continue the circle in whole stitch back stitching when necessary. After putting in the last pin work one more row. Put the coarse pair back over the pillow and sew out all the other pairs and tie them three times. (It is easier if this is done starting from the side where there is one pair of runners). Replace all the pins. (The three pairs on the outer edge of the circle can be used for the main outline). Make a bunch with the remaining five pairs and cut off the coarse threads.

The Main Outline (2)

Part One: Sew in three more pairs besides the pairs saved from the inner circle and hang a coarse pair on a pin. As this first section widens add one more pair on the outside edge. Work the half stitch vein where indicated by twisting the runners once before the odd central downright pair with which a half stitch is made.

Sections 2, 3, 4 and 5 are made consecutively only ending by sewing out at the end of section 5 into the central circle. Tie at the points of each section. Turn the corners back stitching at the last hole on the left, and work to hole A. (diag 17) Sew in the edge pair and tie them three times. (They are no longer needed). Sew the runners which made the last row into the same hole, but now whole stitch these through one pair to their left and tie once. Whole stitch through two more pairs. Leave the runners take the pair to their right whole stitch to hole B and sew them in and tie once. Lay back the pair inside the coarse thread.

Whole stitch the sewn pair to the left through three pairs, leave them and take the pair to their right to hole C, sew them in and tie once, lay back the pair inside the coarse pair. Take the sewn pair to the back stitch and back stitch once more. Whole stitch to hole D, sew in and tie once. Work back through two pairs and leave the runners work the pair beside them to hole E sew them in and tie once. Also at E sew in one new pair. (Needed for an edge pair). Twist them three times and leave them. Whole stitch through the first pair of downrights and tie the runners once then whole stitch to the back stitch and make up the edge stitch here this time. Whole stitch to F and make the usual edge stitch before working the next row untwist the runners at the far side (where the back stitch was) and weave the coarse thread over and under through them so that it lies at the end of the row. Until the two braids become separate, sewings will be made on this side. When they separate a pair of runners will be sewn in to make the edge stitches on the outside edge.

N.B. The instructions for turning are given for five holes along the inner circle. In a few sections there are only four holes in which case the step at hole B will be omitted. Half stitch veins are made in all sections but a two twist vein is either side of this in sections 5 and 8.

Part Two: This is worked in the same way as Part One and is started beside the start for section one sewing in five pairs and hanging the coarse pair in on a pin.

Section 9 is made by sewing in six pairs to section 3 and hanging a coarse pair on a pin. The first scallop has a two twist vein, the second one no vein and the third a half stitch vein, the fourth no vein and the last one a two twist vein. (One extra pair will be needed for the half stitch vein).

Fillings

The fillings used are Toad in the Hole and variations of Toad in the Hole and also Whole Stitch Block and Whole Stitch Block Variation.

Leave all the pins in each filling for one or two days before removing them to allow the stitches to set.

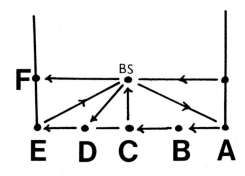

Diagram 17

PRICKING FIVE

LEAF CIRCLE PATTERN (120 thread)

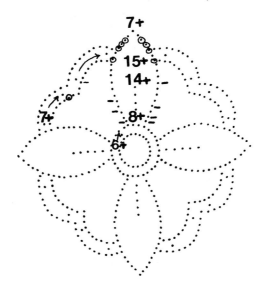

Diagram 18

Central ring (see diagram for central circle pattern 3)   Place a pin in hole 1 on the outer edge of the ring. Hang on six pairs of bobbins. Four unknotted on the right and two on the left with their knotted bobbins overlapping in the centre. Put in a magic thread as described in Pattern one. Twist all the pairs twice. Place the coarse pair over the one pair on the left, under the three central downright pairs and over the two pairs on the right and leave at the back of the pillow. Commence the first row on the right hand side by making a whole stitch with the first two pairs and twist them both three times. Continue in whole stitch to within the last pair. twist the runners making the row three times, place a pin under them in hole 2. make a whole stitch with this and the last pair and twist them both three times. Bring down the coarse thread on this side between the two pins and put inside the two pairs on the left and the one pair of runners on the right. Whole stitch through two pairs to the right and leave the runners. Take the pair to their left and whole stitch through the one pair to their left, twist three times and put a pin in hole 3. Make a whole stitch with the edge pair and twist both pairs three times. Work the first whole stitch of the row and tie the runners once before working the rest of the row to hole 4. (This prevents a large hole on this side where there is a right angle). Work the rest of this central ring back-stitching on the inner edge where necessary to keep the work at the correct angle. Work one last row after putting in the last pin. Cut off the course thread and sew out the other six pairs, two pairs per hole, (one in each side bar) and tie them three times. Use the magic thread for the outer hole. Replace all the pins and bunch the pairs by crossing the extreme edge pair on each side under the other four pairs. Then take one bobbin from each side and tie three times over the top and repeat with the second bobbins. Cut all the pairs off.

Leaves   Begin at the point with seven pairs and a coarse pair, and work in whole stitch. Start adding pairs on each side where indicated in the diagram. Increase to fifteen pairs and a coarse pair at the widest part and take out one pair before commencing the twisted vein in the centre of the leaf. This is made by making six whole stitches twisting the runners once and making six more whole stitches to the end of the row. (ie twisting the runners once in the centre of the downright pairs) On the next row twist twice in the centre and on the third and subsequent rows twist three times. Reverse this to close the vein near the bottom of the leaf. Take out a pair at each hole indicated on the diagram and reduce to eight pairs and a coarse pair at the bottom. Cut off the coarse pair and sew in all the pairs starting on the side with the one pair of runners. Tie all the pairs three times, replace the pins and make two bunches with four pairs of bobbins in each. Cut off all the bobbins. Make the other three leaves in the same way.

Braid Scallop.   Sew in seven pairs of bobbins at the side of the leaf. Hang a coarse pair on a pin behind this and lay in position, inside two pairs on the inside of the scallop and one pair on the outside. Work the first row from the inside to the outside. back stitch where necessary to keep the work level.

Half Stitch Vein.   Start this where indicated by the dot in the centre of the braid. Seven pairs of bobbins plus a coarse pair makes three pairs of runners and five downright pairs. To make the vein work two whole stitches, twist the runners once and make a half stitch with the odd pair of downrights then make two whole stitches. This is repeated to the end of the vein and then each row is made entirely of whole stitches. After closing the vein add one pair where indicated to help fill in the point of the scallop. At the point on the inside, work the edge stitch and then the first stitch of the row, tie the runners once to keep the work form pulling away from the pin. Also remove one pair where indicated leaving seven pairs and a coarse pair for the commencement of the half stitch vein. Close this vein and work two or three rows in whole stitch. Make one row after putting in the last pin. Cut off the coarse pair and sew in the other pairs and tie them three times.
Replace the pins, bunch the pairs and cut them off.
Work the other scallops in the same way.

Fillings: The filling worked in the central ring is worked in the same way as the Diamond filling in Pattern one.
Fourpin filling was worked in the other four spaces.

N.B.   When each filling is completed leave the pins in for one or two days to allow the filling to set.

PRICKING SIX

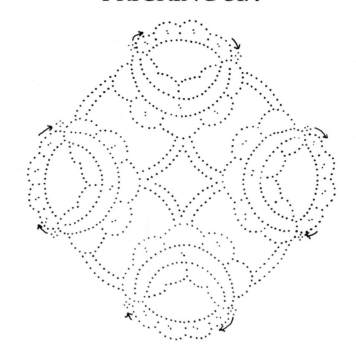

PATTERN 6 (170 thread)

Rose.   Start at the right hand point of the inner most section with six pairs and a coarse pair. Work in whole stitch. Increase as the section widens to eleven pairs and a coarse pair. Reduce to five pairs and a coarse pair and turn the corner and work into the half stitch section. This corner is worked in the same way as the top of the divided leaves in Pattern Two. Increase to seven pairs and a coarse pair as this half stitch section widens and reduce again to five pairs and a coarse pair to turn the corner into the scalloped section. The number of pairs used for these is indicated in diagram 18. Reduce to four pairs and a coarse pair at the end of the last section, sew out and bunch the threads and cut them off.

Sew in seven pairs and hang in a coarse pair on a pin for the half stitch outer edge with purls. Weave the coarse thread through the downrights as usual between the scallops.

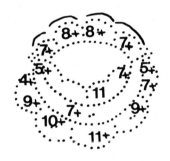

Diagram 19

Variation of Whole Stitch Block filling was used in the flower centre.

Make all four flowers in the same way. When these are completed the whole stitch braids between the flowers can be made. To do this sew in seven pairs into the flower edge and hang a coarse pair in on a pin from behind. Sew out into the next flower at the end of the braid, put the pins back and put the bobbins back between them and over the braid just completed, to bunch them.

Fillings can then be made in the spaces between the flowers and also in the centre.

N.B.   When the fillings have each been completed leave the pins in for one or two days to allow the filling to set.

DIAMOND

Sew a pair of bobbins each side of a pinhole above A and B. Twist them three times and put a pin between them. as A and B.

With the pairs from A, make a leadwork to reach as far as hole 1. Twist three times and put a pin between them. Before putting these to one side tuck the weaver into one of the cover cloths to prevent it from pulling the leadwork out of shape.

With the two pairs at B make a leadwork to reach to hole 2, twist both pairs three times and put a pin between them in hole 2.

Take the right-hand pair from 1 and the left-hand pair from 2 and make a whole stitch and three twists. (No pin).

Take the two left-hand pairs of the four and make a whole stitch and three twists and put a pin between them in hole 3.

Take two right-hand pairs of the four and repeat this putting a pin between them in hole 4.

Take the two centre pairs of the four and make a whole stitch and three twists. (No pin.)

The left-hand two pairs now make a leadwork to reach to C. Twist both pairs three times and put a pin between them in hole C.

The pairs from hole 4 make a leadwork to D, twist them both three times and put pin C between them.

Each group is worked in the same way.

N.B.   It will be noted that it is this filling which is used in the first pattern in the book.

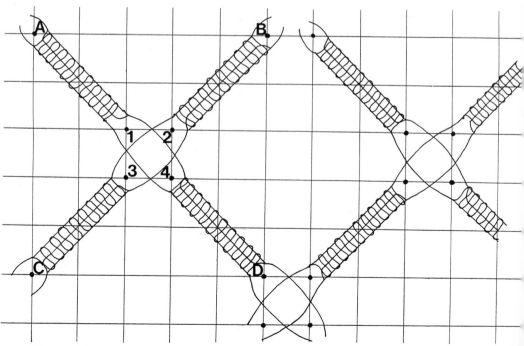

Diagram 20

FOUR PIN

Sew two pairs at an angle, above the top two holes of the pattern. With the left hand two pairs make a whole stitch, twist both pairs three times and put a pin between them in hole 1. fig 70

   With the right hand two pairs, make a whole stitch, twist both pairs three times and put a pin between them in hole 2. fig 71

   Take the centre two pairs of the four, make a whole stitch and twist both pairs three times, but do not put in a pin. fig 72

   Take the left hand two pairs, make a whole stitch, twist both pairs three times and put a pin between them in hole 3. fig 70

   Take the right hand two pairs, make a whole stitch, twist both pairs three times and put a pin between them in hole 4. fig 71

   Take the two centre pairs and make a whole stitch and twist both pairs three times but do not put in a pin. This completes the four holes. fig 72

   The two pairs from 4 pass to hole 1 to the right and the two pairs from hole 3 to hole 2 to the left.

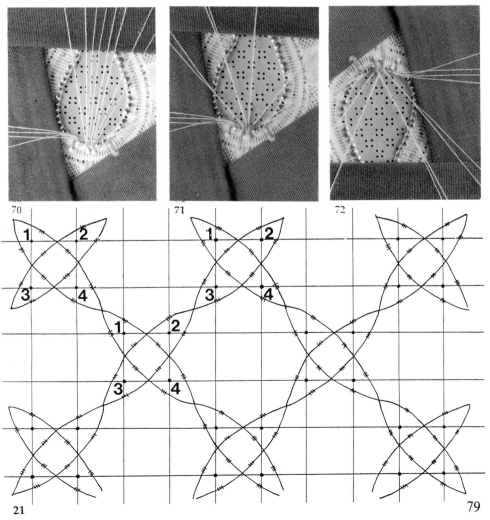

FOUR PIN FLOWER AND LEADWORK

Sew two pairs above hole A and three pairs above the other holes along the top of the filling.

Make a whole stitch and twist both pairs three times with the two pairs from A. Put the pin between them and enclose the pin with a whole stitch.

With the two left-hand pairs from B, make a whole stitch twist them three times and put a pin between the pairs.

Enclose the pin with a whole stitch.

Take pair 3 through 2 and 1 in whole stitch.

Take pair 4 through pairs 2 and 1 in whole stitch.

Make a whole stitch with the two left-hand pairs, twist them both three times and put pin C between them.

Enclose the pin with a whole stitch.

Make a whole stitch with two right-hand pairs, twist them both three times and put in D between them. Enclose the pin with a whole stitch.

Use the pair left at B and the left-hand pair from E to make a leadwork, first twisting both pairs five times. Make a small, square leadwork and again twist both pairs five times.

Make a whole stitch with the two right-hand pair from E to make a leadwork, first twisting both pairs five times. make a small, square leadwork and again twist both pairs five times.

Work the left-hand pair in whole stitch through the two pairs at D.

Next, work four pin flower EFGH in the same way as ABCD. Weave the right-hand leadwork pair through the two pairs at G. The two pairs at D

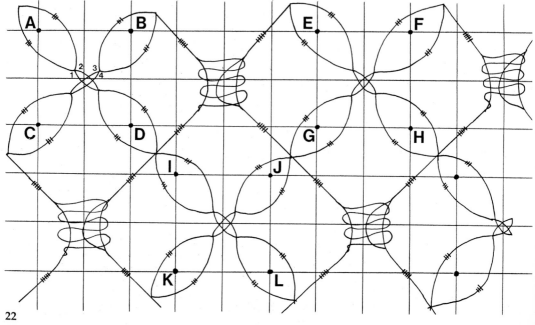

now make a whole stitch and three twists, and pin I is put between them. The same is done with the two pairs from G for pin J.

The rest of the four pin flower is completed in the same way.

The leadwork and flowers alternate in each row.

PIN AND A STITCH

Sew in two pairs above each hole along the filling.

With each two pairs make a whole stitch and twist both pairs three times. Put pin A between them. Enclose the pin with a whole stitch and twist both pairs three times.

Repeat this along the row.

For the second row, take the right-hand pair from A and the left-hand pair from B, make a whole stitch and twist both pairs three times. Put pin C between them and enclose it with a whole stitch and twist both pairs three times.

Leave these two pairs and taking the next two pairs, work them in the same way. (The pairs divide at the bottom of each pinhole and work to the left and right for the next hole).

If a pair is not needed for the second row but could be used again for the third row it is *very* important that this pair should be sewn out at the correct angle and then dropped down a pin's depth before being brought back with three twists to use again. If the pair is not dropped down in this way the angle between the rows will be increased.

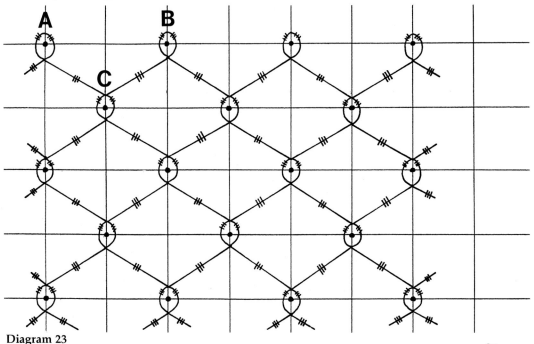

Diagram 23

81

PIN AND A STITCH WITH LEADWORK

The instructions for this filling are the same as for Pin and a Stitch. The diagram is given for the filling to show how the leadworks are made. When pricking this filling it is a good idea to prick all the holes and then mark in the pattern where the leadworks are needed. It will be noted that a leadwork replaces a pinhole. The difference in working here is that only one twist is made before and after the leadwork. if diagonal rows of leadworks are made as in pattern three then the same weaver *must* be used for each leadwork in the diagonal line.

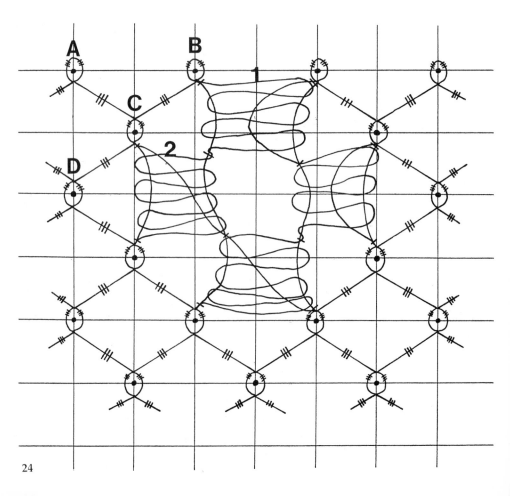

24

TOAD IN THE HOLE

Sew in three pairs diagonally above each hole, except the first one, where only two pairs are needed. With the left-hand pairs from A make a whole stitch and twist once.

With the next two pairs from above hole 2 make a whole stitch and one twist.

Work the far right-hand of these four pairs in whole stitch to the left through the other three pairs, twist seven times and put the pin under them in hole 1. The other holes are all worked in the same way with the same pair of runners.

After hole 6, whole stitch through to the far left and twist both of the left-hand pairs once.

With the two right-hand pairs make a whole stitch and twist once.
Take the pair left at the top of the snatch above hole 2 and twist them five times. Do the same with the pair of their right (Sewn in above hole 1 in snatch B.)

Make a small square leadwork with these two pairs and twist both of them five times at the bottom.

Leave the right-hand pair and take the left-hand pair (which contain the weaver for the leadwork) and, very carefully, whole stitch it through the two right hand pairs from snatch A.

Work snatch B and then the right-hand leadwork pair left hanging can be whole stitched through the left-hand pairs from snatch B.

The remainder of the row is worked in the same way.

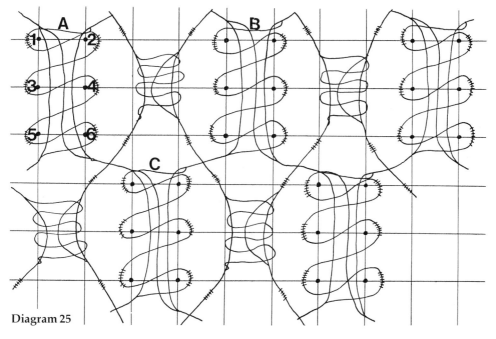

Diagram 25

TOAD IN THE HOLE WITH ENCLOSED PINS

Sew in three pairs daigonally above each hole, except the first one, where only two pairs are needed. With the left-hand two pairs from snatch A, make a whole stitch, twist both pairs three times and put pin 1 between them. Enclose the pin with a whole stitch.

Make a whole stitch with the two left-hand pairs to the right above hole 2, twist them both three times and put pin 2 between them. Enclose the pin with a whole stitch.

The far right-hand pair of the four now works in whole stitch through the three pairs to the left. twist them seven times and put pin 3 under them.

Whole stitch the same pair back to the right through the other three pairs, twist them seven times and pin pin 4 under them and then whole stitch them through to the left.

Take the two left-hand pairs, make a whole stitch and twist both pairs three times. Put pin 5 between them and enclose the pin with a whole stitch.

Take the two right-hand pairs and make a whole stitch and twist both pairs three times. Put pin 6 between them and enclose the pin with a whole stitch.

The pair left hanging above hole 2 of snatch A and the left-hand pair from snatch B are now used for the leadwork. Twist both pairs five times and make a small, square leadwork. twist both pairs five times. The left-hand pair now works carefully through the two pairs at hole 6 of the first snatch.

This is now repeated for the rest of the row. When the next snatch has been worked the right hand leadwork pair can be whole stitched though the two pairs at hole 5 of that snatch.

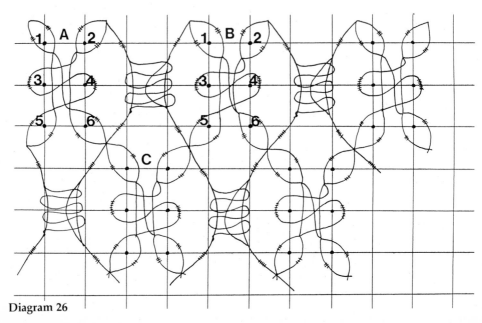

Diagram 26

TOAD IN THE HOLE WITH WIDE LEADWORKS

Sew in two pairs at an angle above each of the holes of the filling.

With each group, make a whole stitch and twist both pairs once. Take the right-hand pair from the four pairs for snatch A and work it in whole stitch to the left through the other three pairs. twist seven times and put pin 1 under them.

Work the same pair in whole stitch to the right through the three pairs, twist seven times and put pin 2 under them. Work in whole stitch through the three pairs to the left twist them three times and put pin 3 under them and leave.

Work the remainder of the row in the same way as far as hole 3.

N.B.   This row has been worked from right to left.

The remainder of the snatch is now made and a pair will have to be sewn in to the edge of the lace in line with hole 3 on the left-hand side.

This pair will now be twisted three times. This pair and the pair left at hole 3 of the nearest snatch will now make a wide leadwork which must fill the space from the edge to pin 3. At the end of the leadwork twist both pairs three times. The left-hand pair will now sew out into the edge and the right-hand pair will whole stitch through the three pairs of the snatch to its right, twist three times and put pin 4 under it.

This pair and the pair from hole three of the snatch to its right now two left-hand pairs. (either three or four half stitches).

Twist them both three times.

The left-hand of these two pairs now very carefully whole stitches through the three pairs to its left, twist seven times and put pin 5 under it. Whole stitch to the right, twist seven times and put in pin 6. Whole stitch through the three pairs to the left. Twist the two left-hand pairs once and make a whole stitch and one twist with the two right-hand pairs.

The remainder of the row is made in the same way. When working the next row the pairs from each snatch divide and work diagonally beneath. Extra pairs will be sewn in as required.

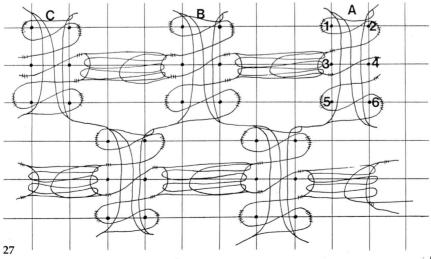

27

TOAD IN THE HOLE VARIATION

Sew in two pairs at A and three pairs at B, C, D etc. across the first row.

With two pairs from A and the two left-hand pairs from B make a half stitch plait. (usually three half stitches with 120 thread and four half stitches with 170)

Make a whole stitch and one twist with the two centre pairs and put pin 1 between them.

Make a whole stitch and one twist with the two left-hand pairs. (No pin)

Make a whole stitch and one twist with the two right-hand pairs. (No pin)

Make a whole stitch and one twist with the two centre pairs and put pin 2 between them.

Again make a whole stitch and twist with the two left-hand and then the two right-hand pairs. (No pin)

Make a whole stitch and twist with the two centre pairs and put pin 3 between.

Make a whole stitch and twist with the two left-hand pairs and with the two right-hand pairs (No pin)

Make a whole stitch and twist with the two centre pairs to enclose the bottom pin.

Two half stitch plaits will now be made with the two right-hand and the two left-hand pairs. (either three or four half stitches).

Twist the pair left at B and the left of the pairs sewn in at C five times. Make a small square leadwork with them, twist five times with them both.

Very carefully whole stitch the left hand pair through the two right-hand pairs from the last block and twist them five times. (They are now ready for a leadwork in the second row).

Make the C, D block in the same way as the first one. The remaining leadwork pair can now be whole stitched through the left-hand two pairs of this second block. Continue in the same way for the remainder of the row.

The pairs now work diagonally to the block below.

WHOLE STITCH BLOCK

Sew two pairs diagonally above each hole in the row.

Take the two left-hand pairs from hole 1 and make a whole stitch and a twist. repeat this with the two pairs above hole 2.

Work the far right-hand pair in whole stitch through the other three pairs in snatch A. Twist seven times and put pin 1 under them.

Work all the holes of the snatch in this way using the same runners.

After putting in pin 6 work through the three pairs to the left. Twist both the left-hand pairs once. With the two right-hand pairs make a whole stitch and one twist.

Work all the other snatches in the row in the same way.

The pairs now work diagonally to the row beneath.

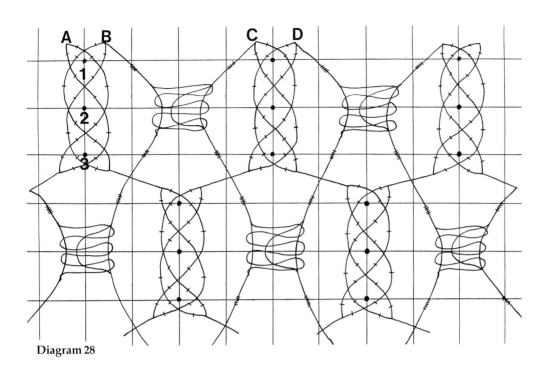

Diagram 28

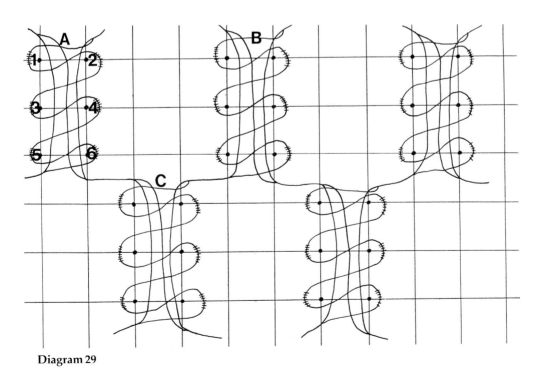

Diagram 29

VARIATION OF WHOLE STITCH BLOCK

Sew two pairs diagonally above each hole in the row. With each two pairs make a half stitch plait of three or four half stitches depending on the thickness of thread being used.

Take the second pair from the right (Of the first four pairs for block A, B), and whole stitch them through the two pairs to their left, twist them seven times and put pin A under them.

Whole stitch the same pair to the right through three pairs, twist them seven times and put pin B under them.

Whole stitch through two pairs to the left. (Just as this pair started off second from the right it is now ending up second from the left).

With the two pairs on the left make a half stitch plait and repeat this with the two pairs on the right.

Work in this way for the remainder of the row.

The pairs divide and work diagonally to the next row beneath.

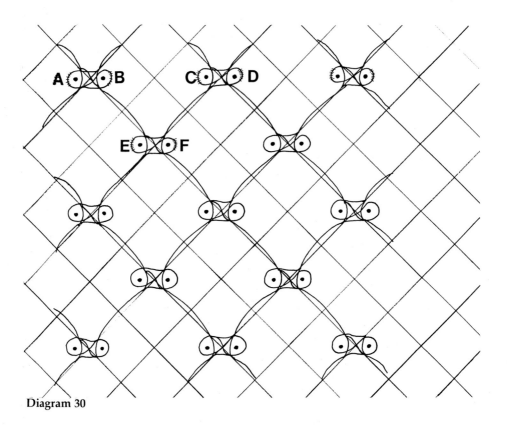

Diagram 30

88

INDEX

SUPPLIERS

Thread, bobbins, cards, books, etc.

Tim Parker.
124 Corhampton Road,
Boscombe East,
Bournemouth,
Dorset. BH6 5NZ

D.H. Hornsby,
149 High Street,
Burton Latimer,
Kettering,
Northants NN15 5RL.
and
25 Manwood Ave.,
Canterbury,
Kent. CT2 7AH

Honiton Lace Shop,
44, High Street,
Honiton,
Devon.

Bobbins only

(Plain and spliced)
Malcolm Thorpe,
36 Twyford Road,
Ward End,
Birmingham B8 2NJ.

Harry Gates,
"Northwood"
16, Harringcourt Road,
Pinhoe.
Exeter EX4 8PQ

Painted bobbins

Shirley Gates,
"Northwood"
16, Harringcourt Road,
Pinhoe.
Exeter EX4 8PQ

Barry Biggins.
"Greenhill",
Hennock.
Newton Abbot.
Devon TQ13 9QM

Mounts

Doreen Campbell,
"Highcliffe"
Bremilham Road
Malmesbury,
Wilts. SN16 00Q

'Ready to Mount' Frames

Frame-Smith
White House Farm
Church Lane
East Cottingwith
Yorks YO4 4TL

**Please enclose an s.a.e. for
a price list.**

RESOURCES

Lace Guild — Magazine contains details of lace groups and courses and articles on making lace etc.

Classes — All local education authorities run adult classes. Details can be found in local libraries and are often in free papers.

Residential courses — These are advertised in magazines and in the centres' brochures. There are many throughout the country.

Books — In the last ten years many books on lace have become available and can be found in craft sections of good book shops. Most libraries have a selection and will always borrow from other libraries.

Museums — A lot of museums have lace collections. The best known is the Victorian and Albert museum in London. Allhallows Museum at Honiton has a large collection of Honiton lace and also Rougemont House Museum of Costume and Lace at Exeter.

BOOK LIST

Patterns

New designs in Honiton Lace — Perryman and Voysey — Batsford
Honiton Lace Pattern Pack — Luxton — Batsford

Techniques

The Techniques of Honiton Lace — Luxton — Batsford
Honiton Lace Patterns — Luxton — Batsford
Introduction to Honiton Lace — Thompson — Batsford

Design ideas

Many Dover publications
i.e. Designs for Artists and Craftsmen

Reference

Lace — a guide to idenification of old lace types and techniques
       Toomer and Voysey — Batsford
Lace — History and Fashion — Kraatz — Thames & Hudson
Lace — a history — Levey — Victoria & Albert Museum
Bobbin Lace in Photographs — Voysey — Batsford

Organisation

The Lace Guild —   The Hollies, 53 Audnam, Stourbridge, West Midlands DY8 4AE

CONCLUSION

I hope this book will be the beginning of an interest and involvement with a very beautiful and creative craft. Lace takes many forms and this is only one of them, they are very varied and can provide a lifelong fascination. As a hobby lacemaking is absorbing, very fulfilling and is also therapeutic in that it is very relaxing.